FAMILY 2.0

Harness Your Business Principles
To Reboot Your Family in 4 Days

JAY FEITLINGER

TELEMACHUS PRESS

This book is intended to provide you with ideas on how to improve communication and better align your family life to create a more functional environment. Each situation is different and your results may differ from those experienced by the author and presented here.

FAMILY 2.0

Published by Telemachus Press, LLC
http://www.telemachuspress.com

Visit the author's website:
http://www.jayfeitlinger.com

ISBN: 978-1-945330-52-0 (eBook)
ISBN: 978-1-945330-53-7 (Hardback)

Library of Congress Control Number: 2017934768

Self Help / Communication & Social Skills

10 9 8 7 6 5 4 3 2 1

Version 2017.04.11

*TO RACHEL, LEXI AND ELLA
FOR SUPPORTING ME, BELIEVING IN ME AND
GOING ON THIS CRAZY JOURNEY WITH ME.
I LOVE LIFE WITH YOU BY MY SIDE!*

TABLE OF CONTENTS

PREFACE i

INTRODUCTION v
   WHY I WROTE FAMILY 2.0 v
   HOW FAMILY 2.0 IS ORGANIZED vi
   WORKSHEETS vii
   STAY CONNECTED vii

DISCOVERING MY DESTINY 1

   AWAKENING 3
      WHEN WORK MEETS FAMILY 5
      A PROBLEM BIGGER THAN ME 7
      THE MAJOR WAKE-UP CALL 9
      IDENTIFYING THE ESSENTIAL FACTOR 12
      CONSIDERING THE SOLUTION 13
      ESTABLISH GOALS 15
      ASSIGN ACCOUNTABILITY 15
      REVIEW AND REVISE 16
      CONSTRUCTING THE ROADMAP 19
      THE DIVERSE DEFINITIONS OF FAMILY 21
      THE TRUTH ABOUT CHANGE 24

   GETTING READY FOR THE JOURNEY 27
      START BY LOOKING IN THE MIRROR 27
      GET ALIGNED WITH YOUR SPOUSE 31
      PITCH YOUR PLAN WISELY 42
      FAMILY MEMBERS, NOT EMPLOYEES 44
      GET YOUR KIDS TO "BUY-IN" 50

CUSTOMIZING YOUR FAMILY ROADMAP........................ 52

ENVISION THE END RESULT 53

DETERMINE YOUR APPROACH.......................... 55

PICK YOUR FAMILY CATEGORIES....................... 58

CREATE YOUR FAMILY TIMELINE....................... 61

GET THE RIGHT RESOURCES 63

GET IN THE RIGHT MINDSET............................. 65

DAY ONE: THE JOURNEY BEGINS 69

DAY ONE: STEP-BY-STEP................................. 71

THE IDEAL FAMILY ROAD TRIP 71

AN UNSETTLING ARRIVAL................................ 78

START WITH SOMETHING SIMPLE 83

THE DINNER CONVERSATION 86

THE THREE MAIN LEARNING CHANNELS 88

PRESENTING THE TIMELINE............................. 93

PRIVATE NIGHTTIME CONVERSATIONS...................... 101

DAY TWO: REFLECTING ON LESSONS LEARNED............... 111

DAY TWO: STEP-BY-STEP................................ 113

STARTING DAY TWO OFF RIGHT 113

TALKING ABOUT RESPECT............................... 117

WHO'S TALKING 121

THE TOY BOX TECHNIQUE 124

PRESENTING THE TOY BOX 125

CREATING THE REFLECTION BOARDS 128

DAY THREE: REIMAGINING YOUR FAMILY'S FUTURE 149

DAY THREE: STEP-BY-STEP............................... 151

ESTABLISHING THE FRAMEWORK............................. 151

SETTING PARAMETERS..................................... 154

CREATING THE DREAM BOARDS 159
PRESENTING THE DREAM BOARDS......................... 162
ALIGNING YOUR FAMILY GOALS 181
THE FUN PART 186

DAY FOUR: THE FINISHING TOUCHES 195
DAY FOUR: STEP-BY-STEP 197
CLEANING OUT THE TOY BOX............................. 198
WRITING LETTERS FOR THE FUTURE 201
A BLISSFUL TRIP BACK HOME............................. 204

POST-RETREAT: THE LONG-TERM PLAN 213
POST RETREAT: STEP-BY-STEP 215
CREATING YOUR FAMILY GOALS SPREADSHEET 216
REFINING YOUR FAMILY VISION 217
THE FIRST FAMILY MEETING 219
ACCOUNTABILITY IN ACTION............................. 231
DISCUSSING PROGRESS 235
ADDRESSING UNACCEPTABLE EXCUSES.................. 238
MODIFYING YOUR GOALS................................. 242
STICKING WITH IT 244

THINGS TO KEEP IN MIND............................. 249
WHAT I WOULD HAVE DONE DIFFERENTLY 251
DIFFERENT, BRILLIANT STRATEGIES 256
WHAT HAPPENS NOW 262
DECISION TIME 265

ABOUT THE AUTHOR............................. 269

FAMILY 2.0 TESTIMONIALS

"So profound and powerful, I cried openly in an airport when I read this book. I desperately wish Jay wrote this years ago when my own kids were younger. An absolute must-read for every 'busy' parent."
>—**Jay Baer:** Husband, dad to 2 kids, President of Convince & Convert, renowned keynote speaker, and New York Times best-selling author of "Youtility: Why Smart Marketing Is About Help Not Hype"

"Since founding Entrepreneurs' Organization, I've heard the same struggles echoed time and again by countless entrepreneurs: 'We can fix our businesses, but we can't fix our relationships with our spouses and children.' Family 2.0 is the answer for business owners looking to restore their home lives and prioritize their families once again."
>—**Verne Harnish:** Husband, father of 4, and author of "Scaling Up (Mastering the Rockefeller Habits 2.0)"

"I've always believed that the most successful entrepreneurs are those with the strongest home lives and most secure personal foundations—and Family 2.0 is all you need to be one of those people."
>—**Mark Moses:** Married with 2 children, CEO & Founding Partner of CEO Coaching International and best selling author of Make Big Happen

"I had the pleasure to hear Jay speak at our MORE parentrepeneur annual conference. It was amazing to hear a confident entrepreneur be so vulnerable about his personal family story and to see how much value it brought to the other entrepreneurs. It was definitely worth the wait about a year later to read Family 2.0. I strongly recommend this book to families of any type and size to take action and get more out of their family following Family 2.0 roadmap."

—**Amber Anderson:** Co-founder of MORE, an organization that creates family-friendly business networking events and retreats, and Kayson, a business strategy agency. She is also a wife and the proud momma of a special, and very active, little boy.

"I've been a business owner for 18 years and this book literally hit home. Seeking a healthy balance between business, family and personal intentions isn't a new concept for driven, goal oriented entrepreneurs, but having an easy to follow blueprint to help us be purposeful about living our intention is innovative. Family 2.0 was an invaluable resource in helping me reach my family life's full potential. If your family is your #1 priority, and you are struggling to find the best way to have your family feel it, this book is for you!"

—**J.P. Dahdah:** Husband for 8 years, father of 2 children, CEO of Vantage Self-Directed IRAs & President of the Arizona chapter of the Entrepreneurs' Organization

"Jay and I share a circle of friends, and we all started to notice a really positive shift happen with him and his family. We were thrilled when he finally let us in on the secret, and it was even better when we found out we could apply the same process to our own families. We talk about work/life balance all the time, but Jay has taken it to a whole new level. He has created work/life AWESOME."

—**Scott Novis:** Husband of 26 years, father of 3 kids, and Founder & CEO of GameTruck

FAMILY 2.0

Harness Your Business Principles
To Reboot Your Family in 4 Days

PREFACE

Let's face it: You're fed up with your family life.

No, you aren't exactly miserable, but you're definitely not happy either. And it's starting to drive you crazy. Whether it's a lack of communication, respect, or love, something is preventing your family from being truly happy and aligned. It never feels like everyone is on the same page and you've been struggling to get along. You've tolerated it for a long time, but now you're sick of it. You want to create a better life for you and your family. You're ready for something to change. You need a reboot.

You don't want a mediocre family life anymore; you want a family life that's truly fulfilling. You want your family members to get along better, communicate more, and reach their full potential. You're eager to foster a more trusting and loving environment at home. You aspire to have more meaningful relationships with everyone, and to understand each person on a deeper level. More than anything, you want to be excited to go home to your family—especially after a long day of work.

You're tired of settling because you aren't the kind of person who settles. You're the kind of person who strives for greatness and who aims to experience a truly fulfilling life. You're fearlessly ambitious, extremely passionate, and you love overcoming challenges and achieving goals. You do whatever it takes to get to where you want to be, and you decided a long time ago that you won't stop until you get there.

When it comes to your career, I bet this go-getter mentality of yours has gotten you really far. Your endless efforts and resilience have surely rewarded you in the business world. You're probably a successful entrepreneur, business executive, or even a CEO. You have a job you love, you're great at what you do, and you've achieved some noteworthy things. Maybe you've launched dozens of companies, or transformed a startup into an enterprise. Either way, you're a natural when it comes to business. You aren't afraid to lead your colleagues, and you effectively motivate them to become the best they can be. You can solve complex business problems, and you're always finding ways to make things work better.

However, your go-getter mentality is both a blessing and a curse at home. It enables you to recognize your family's true potential and reminds you that things could be better. It motivates you to pursue opportunities and changes that can dramatically improve your family. But this isn't a business—this is your family we're talking about! You can't initiate change in the same way as you would at work. You need to consider your family's thoughts and feelings, and approach the situation differently. And, if I were to guess, this is where you get stuck.

You understand how to tackle challenges at work, but you have *no idea* how to overcome them at home. You can figure out how to start a business and grow a company, but you feel lost when it comes to improving your relationships. You can easily talk about business, but you struggle to communicate your feelings. The business world makes complete sense to you, but family relationships confuse you.

I'm about to change that for you. I'm going to make it possible for you to finally initiate change within your family. Once you're done reading this book, you will have all the insight and skills you need to improve your family life. You'll learn how to communicate with your family more effectively. You'll be able to cultivate a more honest, loving, and respectful family environment. You will even find out how to spend more quality time together so that you can foster more meaningful relationships with each other.

****
"ONCE YOU'RE DONE READING THIS BOOK, YOU WILL HAVE ALL THE INSIGHT AND SKILLS YOU NEED TO IMPROVE YOUR FAMILY LIFE."
****

And I haven't even mentioned the best part yet. You and your family members will be able to accomplish all of this without sacrificing your individual aspirations. I will teach you how to balance your personal, work, and family goals so that every area of your life can be spectacular. You won't need to prioritize or neglect certain areas anymore; they will all combine to become one harmonious lifestyle. It will no longer feel like you're juggling a million commitments; it will just seem like you're having one fluid life experience. This means you won't just have a fulfilling career; you will finally have a fulfilling *life*.

Now I know that dealing with family challenges doesn't come naturally to you like business does. Throughout this book, I use business analogies to help you better comprehend and relate to what I'm talking about. I explain how business lessons you've learned can help you better understand your family. I also point out how you can leverage certain business skills to improve your relationships. Because in reality, you already have what it takes to strengthen your family. You just need to approach things a bit differently.

INTRODUCTION

WHY I WROTE FAMILY 2.0

If you're reading this, you have a story to tell. Maybe you're an entrepreneur who is getting regular guilt trips from your wife and kids about the time you spend away. Or you could be a mom who loves running your business, but sometimes worries that immersion in your work has become a way for you to run away from problems at home. Or maybe you're a concerned friend who has noticed work commitments eroding away a close friend's relationships, and you want to help.

Wherever you fall on the spectrum and whatever your particular story entails, I'm *so* glad you're here. I have felt many of the same emotions and experienced many of the same stressors you have, and I have found a way to move beyond that and enjoy a harmonious life. My goal in writing this book is to help you do the same.

Since each of our situations are unique, I worked hard to make Family 2.0 completely customizable. You can go through the process in one day or four days. You can choose to make a trip out of it, or enjoy it from the comfort of your own home. You can adapt it to any family structure and any set of circumstances. However you choose to tailor the roadmap to you and your loved ones, my promise to you is that this process can help you achieve the balance you've been seeking. Once you're done going through this journey, you won't just have a fulfilling career; you will finally have a fulfilling life.

HOW FAMILY 2.0 IS ORGANIZED

The following pages of this book will take you through my story. I have shared the good and bad with you so you can learn from my mistakes (and hopefully prevent making many of your own). Since I'm an entrepreneur like many of you, I can relate to the specific struggles you face that many may not understand.

Throughout the book, I show you how I took proven business practices and adapted them to my family relationships in order to get big results. You might be surprised that you already have all the skills you need to strengthen your family; you just need someone to walk you through how to use them. I've laid out, in detail, the exact steps you can take on each day of the Family 2.0 retreat. But you can customize this as much as you need to in order to make it work for your own family. I've also included ways to keep the momentum going after you come home, so results will be long-lasting.

I hope my story will resonate with you, and inspire you to start making changes today that can transform you and your family. The best part of the Family 2.0 roadmap is that you don't have to wait to get started. There's no better time than this exact moment to regain balance and rejuvenate your relationships and your life.

You've experienced the problem… and now I'm here to walk you through a solution. Who's ready to jump in with me?

WORKSHEETS

There are 10 different worksheets that are discussed in the book. These will help you initiate important conversations and get the ball rolling toward transformation.

Make sure to visit www.jayfeitlinger.com to download each of the worksheets.

STAY CONNECTED

I would love to hear how Family 2.0 helped you or where you might need some extra support. Here are the best ways to connect with me:

Website: www.jayfeitlinger.com

Email: jay.feitlinger@gmail.com

Twitter: www.twitter.com/jayfeitlinger

LinkedIn: www.linkedin.com/in/jayfeitlinger/

DISCOVERING MY DESTINY

AWAKENING

I didn't discover how to strengthen my family by becoming a family therapist or psychologist. Believe it or not, I found out how to improve my family through my journey as an entrepreneur and a CEO. The extraordinary experiences I encountered along the way opened my eyes to both the problem and the solution. They also dramatically shaped who I am today and changed my family's path forever.

My road to entrepreneurship was like a hidden dirt trail in the middle of a bare Arizona desert or, as I call it, my home state. I didn't come from an entrepreneurial family, and I didn't have an ingenious idea for a new business (at least not initially). In fact, when I made the decision to become an entrepreneur and CEO, I didn't even know that much about how to run a business. I just wanted to take control of my destiny.

In the late 90s, I started working for a telecommunications company known as WorldCom. Shortly after I began working there, I became a successful sales consultant and earned significant commissions. I felt incredibly fortunate for my job and loved working for the company—and most of my coworkers felt the same way. Because I was one of the top sales representatives, I was fortunate enough to be invited to a national business event in Hawaii in 2002. While I was in Hawaii, the notorious downfall of WorldCom began.

Journalists began swarming around the hotel trying to interview anyone who worked at WorldCom. Our company executives told us to avoid communicating with the press because they were trying to cover a negative news story about WorldCom. We weren't given any details about the story though, so all of us were left wondering what was going on. That night when I turned on the news, I sat in complete shock as I listened to reporters explain that my employer was in serious financial trouble. It completely caught me off guard, and I had no idea what it would mean for my career at WorldCom.

When I got back from the business event, my coworkers were just as confused and in the dark as I was. Fear and uneasiness was spreading throughout the workplace because our executives weren't answering our questions. Soon enough, everything at the company started falling apart. Thousands of WorldCom employees lost their jobs, and our CEO Bernie Ebbers resigned. I was fortunate enough to avoid getting laid off, but the next few months were heartbreaking and chaotic. Then, on July 22, 2002, the national news broke that WorldCom filed the largest bankruptcy in corporate history. At that point, my personal wealth took a major hit as I had hundreds of thousands of dollars invested into the WorldCom stock.

After losing all of my investments and hope in WorldCom, I needed to reconsider what I was doing with my life. I realized that working for other people meant giving up control over my own destiny, and that was a very unsettling feeling that I just couldn't swallow. I decided that I wanted to be the director of my own life. But in order for that to happen, I would need to become an executive or CEO of a company. I began exploring all the ways I could make this happen, and then chose my most practical path: I became a franchise owner.

While owning a franchise was definitely more challenging than I could've ever expected, it proved to me that I was born to be an entrepreneur and business owner. Over the course of the next 20 years, I launched eight different businesses—some of which were major successes, while others were absolute failures. But whenever anything went wrong with my companies, I committed myself to pushing through it and moving on. I wasn't going to let failure hold me back from achieving lasting success. Instead, I would learn from the failures and apply that knowledge to my next venture. Plus, when you're born to be an entrepreneur, quitting really doesn't feel like an option.

WHEN WORK MEETS FAMILY

Although I experienced uncertainties as I pursued my new career path, one thing in my life became more certain than ever. Throughout all of my entrepreneurial pursuits, my wife Rachel was more supportive than I could have ever fathomed. Even when I failed multiple times in a row and she would have been completely justified in losing all hope in me, she never once did. She was always there beside me, encouraging me to do what I love. All of her actions and emotional support verified to me that, without a doubt, I married the right woman.

A few years after I became an entrepreneur, Rachel and I had two daughters. Our daughter Ella is currently 10 years old, and our daughter Lexi is 12 years old. They are as sweet and loving as young children can be, so I'm aware that I'm a very lucky father. However, they certainly aren't perfect angels and we definitely have our challenges. Ella and Lexi are almost polar opposites. Ella is very shy and sensitive, while Lexi is very outspoken and confident. As a result, they communicate differently and fight often.

Even though Ella and Lexi are very different, they still have several similarities. For example, both of them have a very difficult time understanding why I work so much. I've explained plenty of times before that I work in order to provide for our family, but this answer is never good enough for them. No matter what I say, they still believe that I shouldn't work as much as I do. This is another challenge we often deal with. I've always known that my daughters hated how much I work, but I really didn't think there was anything I could do about it.

I believed that the harder I worked, the more benefits I would get. I would try to reply to a few emails before and after dinner, and I would plan out my to-do list for the next day while I got ready for bed. I believed that these workaholic habits of mine would ultimately benefit my family, so naturally Rachel and the girls should be okay with it. But if you're constantly on the go and never "in the moment," you're eventually going to run into problems.

Not surprisingly, working nonstop altered my personality. I would always come home tired and stressed after work, causing me to be very disgruntled and negative at home. And as you probably know from your own personal experiences, negative energy is contagious. When I'm cranky at home, my daughters witness it and become irritable too. Eventually, everyone in the house is in a bad mood for no good reason. We all get upset about petty things, and start arguing just for heck of it. Then somebody raises their voice, and somebody else raises their voice even louder. It just turns into this vicious cycle that isn't enjoyable or healthy for anyone. *Can you relate?*

Eventually, Rachel brought this pattern up to me in her typical not-so-subtle way. She flat-out told me that she didn't like the path our family was on. She said she missed spending time with me, felt like we were more like roommates than spouses, and revealed that she was feeling neglected. She also *hated* all of the fighting and yelling that went on in our home. Considering that she's always accepted my busy work life and doesn't ask much more of me (e.g. household chores or errands for the kids), these honest comments really weighed on me. I had to stop and ask myself, "When I'm finally a CEO of a large and successful company, will I have my family with me to share my success?" I couldn't *bear* to accept that the answer could be "no." What's the point of success if I don't have a family to share it with?

A PROBLEM BIGGER THAN ME

As time went on, it became more obvious to me that my family problems were real—and I didn't need to solve them just for myself. I spent a lot of time networking with other entrepreneurs, and I began to notice a trend: many entrepreneurs struggle with how to communicate with their family members or make time for them. In fact, I'm sure most of them would agree that maintaining a happy family is more challenging than running a successful business.

Most of these entrepreneurs that I met were from Entrepreneurs' Organization (EO), of which I've been a member since 2011. Joining the group was one of the best decisions of my life mostly because the organization allowed me to finally get the support I needed. As you probably know, being an entrepreneur can be a very lonely existence. If you don't have any business partners, you often feel isolated and sometimes even hopeless. I knew that if I didn't get the support I needed, especially in the beginning, my career as an entrepreneur would be a very desolate place. Fortunately, once I joined EO, I gained access to all of the business advice I could ask for. But when I asked other entrepreneurs for *family* advice, the responses were very different.

About three years ago, I told a story at my EO group about a fight I had with Lexi. She was stressing out about a school test coming up, and she didn't feel like I was helping her enough. I tried to explain that things had been crazy at work, but my excuses just made her angrier. The argument escalated into a ridiculous fight, so I felt like I had no other choice but to send Lexi to her room. About five minutes after she slammed her bedroom door closed, I heard the front door open. When I looked out the front window, I saw my very small daughter storming off with a big, clunky suitcase. It was amusing at first, but then my "Dad mode" kicked in. She was in her pajamas, wearing no shoes, and it was about 10:30 at night. I opened the door and secretly followed her as she walked down the street. After walking a few blocks, she sat down on a curb. I could tell she was really sad and upset, but I wasn't sure what to say or do, so I just stayed silent and hidden. Eventually she headed back home, and went directly into her room. I didn't talk to her at all that night.

When I shared this story, everyone laughed. Then other people exclaimed, "My son (or daughter) did the same thing a couple years ago!" Almost everyone could relate to the situation, but nobody could give me advice about what I should do with Lexi. I was honestly taken aback—and even a little frightened. We all have these problems with our families, and we constantly complain about them, but *nobody is offering any solutions!*

I came to the conclusion that if I wanted to solve these issues with my family, I would need to figure it out on my own—just like I had to do with all of my business issues. But this issue was beyond my field of expertise and sadly I kept pushing it off.

THE MAJOR WAKE-UP CALL

Fortunately, one very small yet significant experience propelled me into action.

It was a Friday night, and Ella asked me if I would swim in our pool the next day. I figured I had the time, so I said yes. She started dancing around the room with excitement and exclaimed, "Yaaaay, I can't wait!"

The next day, I woke up early so I could get some work done before Ella got up. I was deep into my work when Ella finally walked into my office. She was already wearing her swimsuit.

"Are we still going to the pool, Daddy?!" She eagerly asked. I was right in the middle of something, so I was pretty irked. I really wanted to finish what I was doing before I took her to the pool.

"Yeah Ella, of course," I responded. "Can you just give me five more minutes? I'm right in the middle of something."

"Okay ..." She replied. I told her thank you as she walked out of the room, and then I jumped back into my work. I could tell by the look on her face that she had heard this excuse far too often.

Exactly five minutes later, Ella walked back into my office. And I won't lie—I was immediately agitated when I saw her. I was still working on something and I had no desire to stop.

"It's been five minutes! Are you ready?" Ella stated.

"I'm sorry Ella, but I still need more time. Just give me another five minutes," I replied.

"Seriously, Daddy? Ugh, alright ..." She glared at me and then stomped off. I thought about getting up and running after her, but I couldn't get myself to do it. I *really* wanted to finish what I was working on.

So, I just kept working.

About fifteen minutes later, I could hear Ella walking back. I spun around in my office chair as soon as I registered the sound of her footsteps. I figured she must be really mad at me by this point, especially since I didn't run after her. But when she finally walked in, she didn't seem angry at all. Instead, she just looked really sad...

Ella slumped into Rachel's office chair across from me, still wearing her swimsuit. The reality of what I had done started to sink in. I felt like a terrible father.

Before I could start apologizing, Ella asked, "Daddy, why are you always working so much?"

"Umm … Well, I've explained this to you before Ella," I began. I was nervous to say the wrong thing. "I work so that I can pay for our house—and for our food, vacations and the cars. And so we can do all of the fun things that we want to do!"

"How much money do you make in an hour?" She asked next. This really caught me off guard, mainly because I had no idea she understood about being paid. At the time, she was only nine years old! I also didn't have an exact answer for her, but I figured I could provide a rough estimate.

"Umm … I make about $200 an hour," I answered.

She scribbled on a piece of paper. Then she asked, "Okay, can I borrow $140?" I didn't understand what she was getting at.

"Why do you need $140, Ella?" I replied.

"Well, I have sixty dollars saved up right now. So if I can borrow $140, then I can buy an hour with you," she explained.

As soon as I processed what Ella said, I was beyond speechless. I went from busy work mode to "I feel like I'm going to cry" mode. My own daughter felt like she needed to pay me in order to get time with me, and that just wasn't right. Why was I prioritizing my work over my family? And why was I getting angry with my completely innocent daughter for wanting me to stop? I realized I was being a terrible father, and I hated myself for it. That was the pivotal moment when I decided that something needed to change.

****
"MY OWN DAUGHTER FELT LIKE SHE NEEDED TO PAY ME IN ORDER TO GET TIME WITH ME, AND THAT JUST WASN'T RIGHT."
****

IDENTIFYING THE ESSENTIAL FACTOR

Although I knew I needed to do something about this problem, I initially had no idea how I was going to do it. Fortunately, solving problems is one of my favorite things to do. I thought to myself, "If I can solve complex business problems, I *must* be able to solve complex family problems." And that's when I got the idea—what if I could apply the lessons I've learned from the business world to my family life?

I started to contemplate all of the business lessons I've learned over the years, and I made a list of the ones that could be applicable to my family. Most importantly, I assessed why certain businesses I launched were more effective than others.

ShopTab was one of my first successful businesses, so I considered the different steps I took when launching it. If you haven't heard of ShopTab, do you remember when Facebook had tabs on top of the business pages? It is a social commerce app that allowed eCommerce businesses to monetize their efforts on Facebook and build a store within their page. Before launching ShopTab with my business partner and close friend Bret Giles, I met with several eCommerce professionals to get their advice on how to make my product operate best. I also interviewed dozens of small business owners to ensure that there was truly a need for ShopTab. These conversations provided me with tons of valuable information that allowed us to make ShopTab successful.

I never took these steps when I was launching my previous businesses, which now I understand was a huge mistake. If I had communicated more effectively with relevant professionals and interested buyers, my success rate for launching businesses would probably be much higher. But effective communication isn't only valuable for business.

When I really thought about it, other failures in my life could have been avoided if I had communicated more effectively too.

For instance, consider the fight that happened between Lexi and me. When she came back home after "moving out," I should have gone into her room, apologized for raising my voice, and really listened to her concerns. If I took the time to understand her thoughts and needs, there's a good chance we could talk it out and resolve the problem. But because I didn't talk to her and I had no idea what was going on in her head, I couldn't determine a solution. Once this reality hit me, I felt like a fool for not realizing it sooner. It's incredibly clear to me now that without effective communication, relationships can't reach their full potential.

CONSIDERING THE SOLUTION

After taking this all in, I knew I needed to create some sort of plan or roadmap that would help my family effectively communicate and coexist. That's when I started to imagine what it would be like if my family communicated the same way that my team at StringCan Interactive did. StringCan Interactive is a digital marketing agency in Scottsdale, Arizona that I founded back in 2010. I am currently the CEO of the company, and I'm extremely proud of where it stands today. Our inbound marketing approach still remains unique, we produce quality work and results for our clients, and our revenue is steadily growing.

However, I honestly believe that StringCan wouldn't be where it is today if it wasn't for the culture that my team and I created. My employees and I value communication more than anything else, and we are completely honest with one another. I share my concerns and financial updates with every team member, which gives them unique insight into the organization. Sure, my transparency makes me more vulnerable, but this approach is extremely effective with the right team members. I find that it allows us to get through business hurdles and internal conflict a lot faster—and as a team. This vulnerable and transparent culture also makes it easier for anyone to admit when they need additional help or support. As a result, everyone is able to stay happy and successful in their role.

I'm incredibly fortunate for my team's communication skills and our company culture, because it wasn't always this way. There was a point in time when my employees often fought with each other, avoided hard conversations, and even lied to my face. And occasionally, these situations still do happen. But over the years, I found ways to strengthen our communication and culture so that these internal conflicts could be mitigated.

As soon as I recalled this situation with my employees, I had a very uplifting and eye-opening thought: If I was able to get a team of people to better communicate and coexist, shouldn't I be able do the same for my family?

I considered how I transformed my employees at StringCan into a high-functioning team. I considered all of techniques and procedures that I tested out, and pinpointed which ones were the most effective. Without a doubt, I knew there was one business process that was more valuable than all of the others: our annual goals planning activity.

ESTABLISH GOALS

Every year, my team members and I get together to determine our goals for StringCan for the next year. Prior to meeting, I present my vision for the next year and ask everyone to prepare their ideas on how to reach the vision and a list of company gaps that they believe are hindering our company's success. These gaps can relate to the company as a whole or the employee's specific role. After they've completed this task, we have a meeting to review everyone's ideas and gaps. When we did this in 2015, we initially had a long and overwhelming list of 74 gaps. We pinpointed which gaps were most relevant and aligned to the same unified vision for the next year's success. This allowed us to narrow the list down to 16 critical gaps to solve over the next year.

ASSIGN ACCOUNTABILITY

As the next step in the process, we determine the most practical solutions for each of these 16 critical gaps. Finally, we assign a team member to each gap. This team member doesn't necessarily need to solve the gap; they are just required to oversee the gap and ensure that steps are being taken to resolve it. Then, once a month, we meet to review our progress on each gap and bring up any concerns we have.

REVIEW AND REVISE

My team looks forward to this process every year because they see it as an opportunity to make our team stronger and better. And by the end of the following year, almost all of the gaps we focused on are successfully resolved. Of course, we sometimes need to modify them a bit or rethink the solution. But in the end, *this process always works!*

Because we identify and resolve all of gaps that are holding us back, StringCan is able to significantly improve and grow every year. We are able to continue making progress on our business goals and work toward attaining our ultimate business vision. This allows not only our business to be more successful, but also all of us as individuals. By understanding how to recognize roadblocks and overcome them, we strengthen our problem-solving skills and maintain an attitude of perseverance. These traits empower us to improve ourselves every day and accomplish almost anything we desire to.

There are a few reasons why I think our annual goals planning activity is incredibly effective. First of all, during our initial meeting to discuss our gaps and pinpoint the most critical ones, I make sure that everyone participates. Even though it's my business and I may *think* I know what gaps and goals we should be focusing on next year, I could be completely off-base. Maybe what I think matters really doesn't matter at all, or maybe I'm unaware of a huge problem that nobody has mentioned to me yet. My employees see different opportunities and problems within the company than I do, especially because their responsibilities and needs drastically differ from mine. By understanding what gaps they experience and consider to be most detrimental, I can more accurately determine what gaps have the most significant impact on our team.

After we choose what gaps to focus on, we brainstorm *as a team* how to best overcome them. While I could come up with solutions myself, sometimes my employees have better ideas than I do. They also foresee problems or raise concerns that I don't always consider. By collaborating on the solutions together, I can avoid initiating change that may cause issues or resentment. We are also more likely to determine the most effective ways to overcome our gaps when we work together.

I also believe that consistently meeting to track our progress is a key factor in our success. First of all, these meetings serve as a reminder that our gaps still exist and must be overcome. This prevents us from ignoring lingering roadblocks within our organization and pushes us to stay accountable for overcoming them. Otherwise, we would devote less time and attention to them because "more important" work tasks come up. While supporting our clients is certainly our top priority, that doesn't mean we should put off improving our business. Both are critical to our company's success, so both deserve our time and attention. Thanks to the monthly meetings, we are able to remember this and maintain the right mindset. It's so easy to forget what really matters, so having regular reminders helps.

The monthly meetings also motivate us to clearly and honestly communicate about the progress we're making on our goals. As a result, they reinforce integrity and transparency. These traits are critical to a successful workforce, as well as a successful life. Because if we aren't honest with others, and ourselves we are much more likely to compromise our values, hurt others, and hold ourselves back. These behaviors can cause regret, resentment, broken relationships, and self hate. By communicating honestly and openly, we can improve our relationships with others instead of jeopardizing them. Even more importantly, we are able to get support when we need it most.

Ironically enough, I'm usually the one who needs the most help with making progress on our annual goals. A large majority of our goals require executive decisions, like hiring an administrative assistant or finding a new office space, so I end up being responsible for most of them. However, I am stretched thin because I fill multiple roles within our organization (e.g. salesman, recruiter, manager, mentor). As a result, it's extremely challenging for me to make substantial progress on every single gap. Fortunately, my team is very understanding when I admit that I'm falling behind and need help. They don't get upset or disappointed; they either just hold me more accountable or find a way to help me out.

For example, when I admitted that I hadn't even started looking for a new office space, one of my employees offered to conduct research and prepare a list of potential office spaces for us. It was a brilliant idea and saved me hours of time. Once I received the list, I was able to quickly pinpoint which option was the best one. If I hadn't been vulnerable enough to admit that I needed help, I would have never received that level of support. Needless to say, I am always honest with my employees. And I believe it's a major reason why we are a high-functioning team.

CONSTRUCTING THE ROADMAP

As I reflected on the benefits that resulted from the planning process that I implemented at StringCan, I realized that it largely resembled what I desired for my family. More than anything, I wanted my family and I to overcome the obstacles that were preventing us from being as happy and successful as possible. I also aspired for us to communicate more effectively, support each other more often, and work together as a team. If you think about it, StringCan's annual goals planning process achieved these exact outcomes for my business.

****
"WHAT IF, IN ADDITION TO CREATING ANNUAL GOALS FOR MY BUSINESS, I CREATED ANNUAL GOALS FOR MY FAMILY?"
****

What if, in addition to creating annual goals for my business, I created annual goals for my family? Instead of going through the process with my StringCan team, I could complete it with Rachel and my daughters. This way, everyone could contribute and our goals would be customized to our unique needs and desires.

If this process can work for my employees, I didn't see why it couldn't work for my family. Of course, I would need to tweak a couple things so that it's more kid-friendly and family-oriented, but I already had a solid framework that I knew was effective. So, that's exactly what I did. I used the framework from this process to create a customized roadmap for my family. I call it the Family 2.0 Roadmap because it was designed to help reboot my family to become closer, happier, and more successful. Once I finished creating this roadmap and asked my family to complete it with me, I walked them through each step. And thankfully, the results were spectacular.

Ever since my family began following this roadmap, we have been more loving and cooperative than ever before. We've addressed and resolved some major family issues that felt impossible to overcome in the past—including the constant fighting. Of course, we aren't perfect, and avoiding fights will always be somewhat of a struggle for us. But now when we have arguments, it rarely escalates into yelling or hurtful remarks. We are much better at remaining calm, and we remember to communicate how we feel. Often times, we're even able to agree on a reasonable solution or compromise in under five minutes.

In addition to communicating more effectively and more often, we are supporting each other on an entirely new level. Instead of just being there for each other when it's desperately needed, we are regularly motivating one another to perform our best, to enjoy every moment of each day, and to live a well-balanced life. As a result, we push each other to be successful without nagging or being passive aggressive about it like before. We still hold each other accountable, but now we are able to do it in a positive and loving way.

Ever since we embraced this roadmap, I've been spending less time overworking myself and investing more time into my hobbies and health too. I finally figured out how to balance all of the different priorities within my life so that I can make everyone—including myself—truly happy. I am so much more peaceful as a result, and I sleep significantly better at night. Now I feel more refreshed and energized than I ever did, which is allowing me to accomplish more than I ever did before.

As far as my relationship with my wife, it feels like we've closed the gap that started to form between us. We no longer take each other for granted, and we explain how appreciative we are for one another more often. If we are ever upset about something, we calmly communicate how we feel instead of being passive aggressive about it or keeping it all in. This allows us to solve problems as soon as they arise so that issues don't linger within our relationship. We do the same with our daughters as well, along with our friends, co-workers and other family members.

Now that our family isn't focusing on negative or insignificant details, the amount of love, peace, and joy that exists within our home is unbelievable. I enjoy being at home now, and I no longer get anxiety when I'm spending quality time with my family. This roadmap has taught me how to balance my priorities and be *in the moment*, so I can finally relax without worrying about falling behind when I do.

THE DIVERSE DEFINITIONS OF FAMILY

Initially, I didn't intend to encourage other families to follow the Family 2.0 Roadmap I created. But when I began to tell my entrepreneurial friends about my experience, they were all interested in learning more about it. They wanted to know how the roadmap worked and if they could take their own families through it. My first reaction was, "Yes!" I didn't see why this roadmap wouldn't work for their families too. All they needed to do was modify certain parts of the roadmap so that it would be appropriate and effective for their family.

Eventually, many of my friends did follow this roadmap. And every single one of them reached out to me afterward to tell me all about their experience. One of my friends said that his family was finally able to find common ground, even though they all have completely different hobbies and personalities. Another friend of mine said she learned how to talk and relate to her children, so now she's having meaningful conversations with them. The feedback that shocked me most was from a close friend of mine. He said that this roadmap completely eliminated his tunnel vision, which he didn't even know he had. He understands his life differently and more clearly now, and he's a thousand times happier because of it.

Even though none of my friends' families resemble mine, this roadmap still improved their families in some way. They were also able to modify it as they saw fit, which made the roadmap even more effective. This verified to me that this roadmap can benefit almost any family—including yours. If you are wondering, "Will this roadmap really work for *my* family?" I can confidently say, "Yes!"

Because the roadmap is entirely customizable, it can work for almost any family. No matter what your family looks like or how you define family, this roadmap is right for you.

Let's say you have three or more children, as well as a couple stepchildren. Or maybe you live with cousins, grandparents, grandchildren, aunts or uncles. Can they all still participate? Sure! However, I would suggest only including the family members that you live with or see on a daily basis. Having discussions and making decisions will be more difficult and time-consuming if numerous people are involved. For the sake of your own personal sanity, invite as few family members as possible.

If you and your spouse don't have any children, you two can still follow and benefit from this roadmap too. In fact, I'm sure the first part of this roadmap will be much faster and easier without kids! I honestly wish I followed this roadmap with my wife 14 years ago before we got married and had kids. As you will find out later on, I spent a lot of time helping and explaining things to my daughters as we completed each activity. This won't be the case for you though, so you will be able to spend less time giving instructions and assisting others. In fact, you may not even need to complete the activities at all. If you don't believe that hands-on activities will be worthwhile for you and your spouse, you can just have honest conversations and thoughtful discussions to complete each part of the roadmap.

Maybe you do have children, but they have full-time jobs and no longer live at home. While you may be thinking it's too late for your family to follow this roadmap, that's not true. It is never too late. *There is no better time than now to chase happiness.* In fact, this roadmap can be especially valuable for you because it will allow you to spend more quality time with your children. Even they are often too busy or don't live nearby, this roadmap will teach your children how they can make time for you and thoroughly enjoy every moment of it. Additionally, you will learn how to better communicate and support each other as grown adults.

Clearly, this roadmap is appropriate for all types of families. But there is one small caveat... If any of your children are younger than seven years old, pursuing this roadmap will be more difficult. Your children also won't get as much value out of it because they will be too young to fully comprehend everything. In order to successfully follow this roadmap, your children must have basic motor skills and be able to hold a conversation. They should also be able to think critically as well as creatively. If your children aren't at this level of development yet, I highly encourage you to wait until they are before getting them involved in this roadmap. In the meantime, follow this process solely with your significant other. This way, you and your spouse will be truly aligned by the time you get the kids involved—and this will make everything go much more smoothly.

THE TRUTH ABOUT CHANGE

If you would have told me two years ago that I could dramatically improve my family life, I wouldn't have believed you for a second. For years, I thought that there was nothing I could do to change the path that my family and I were on. Trust me, I tried all sorts of parenting techniques and approaches to prevent the fighting and countless other bad habits we adopted. I think I hit bottom when I found myself thinking we were stuck in our ways and I had no control over our future. Well, now I'm aware that I was dead wrong. It wasn't impossible for us to change; I was just trying to initiate change the wrong way.

I'm sure you know exactly what I'm talking about. Think about a time when you've told your kids or spouse that you're finally going to take on an entirely new habit or hobby—like reading books or going to the gym. But then other priorities come up, and you don't follow through with what you said. Eventually, you commit to it again later on, and this time *you really mean it*! You finally pursue your new goal and manage to make some progress—but this progress doesn't last.

Why does this happen? Why do we say we're going to do certain things but then we never do them? Is it because we don't have enough time, or maybe we just don't care enough to actually make it happen? Sometimes, yes, that's exactly why. But more often than not, the real reason is because we underestimate how much effort is required to change our routines and habits. We *say* we're going to make it happen (and we *really* mean it this time!) but that's only one of the many steps required to effectively implement change. No matter how badly you want to change yourself or your family, it won't happen unless you seriously think it through with those who matter and create a game plan, together, for how you will make it happen.

Consider what happens when you initiate a major change within a business. Let's say you decide to start offering a new product or service, or maybe you want to drastically change a standard business procedure. Before you make this decision, you would most likely get your key stakeholders together and talk it through.

As you discuss the change, you would ask the following questions:

- Will this change benefit our business?
- How beneficial will it be?
- Does this change align with our business strategy and goals?
- What potential problems could arise as a result of this change?
- Can we resolve those problems if they arise?
- Do the benefits of this change outweigh the disadvantages?

- How will this change impact every area of our business?
- How will this change impact our employees?

Once you are finally ready to implement the change, you don't just casually mention it to your team. Instead, you most likely announce the change to everyone that it will impact during a company meeting. In this meeting, you also clearly explain why you decided to make this change so that your team understands your rationale. Then you ask if anyone has questions, and you address any concerns that are brought up.

In the following weeks, you begin to implement the change. But it's probably executed in a number of phases, and each phase is carefully carried out. Once the change is fully implemented, you begin to measure and track its results. This way, you can ensure that the change is effective and produces the benefits you expected.

When a major change occurs within a business, it's a big deal. Multiple people are involved and a strategic plan is put together because the change *must* be worthwhile and executed correctly. Otherwise, the change will cost the business valuable amounts of time and money for no legitimate reason. And in the business world, that's a tragedy.

Can you imagine if we treated change within our personal and family lives the same way? What if we told the people who cared about us the most that we wanted to make a specific change? What if we understood how this change would impact every area of our lives before committing to it? What if we announced the change out loud to those who would be the first to witness it, and then we carefully executed the change?

If this was how we treated change in every area of our lives, we would be significantly more successful. I know this for a fact because that's exactly what this roadmap did for my family. We thoroughly discussed and decided what changes we wanted to make, created a game plan for how we would accomplish them, and then we carefully and successfully implemented the changes. And as you know, the impact these changes had on my family were pretty incredible. Fortunately, this roadmap can help your family accomplish the same thing.

GETTING READY FOR THE JOURNEY

How badly do you want to improve your family? Are you seriously ready to make it happen? Are you committed to creating a more meaningful life for you, your spouse and children? Are you willing to put in the time and effort that's required to improve your reality? Because you see, there's a huge difference between *wanting* to do something and *actually making it happen*. But for some reason, when it comes to entrepreneurs and their families, this distinction tends to be forgotten. But before you can begin, you must take a hard look at yourself in the mirror.

START BY LOOKING IN THE MIRROR

This book isn't about your family. This book is about *you*. Because if you aren't committed to this roadmap, your family won't be either. Before you even mention the idea to your spouse or kids, you need to really look at yourself in the mirror and understand why you want to do this. You need to consider how much your family means to you, and how important it is to you that things get better.

I can't tell you how many times I've listened to my entrepreneurial friends complain about their families. They talk about how angry their husband or wife made them, how annoying their kids are being, or how boring it is to be at home. After describing what they are dealing with, they express how much it bothers them and how badly they want it to change. But whenever I ask, "Then why don't you say something?" they stare at me in absolute terror. "Oh god no, I'd rather put up with it than say how I'm feeling," they reply. "I don't want to start another fight!"

In other words, my friends would rather be unhappy forever than initiate one hard conversation. If you're asking me—that sounds really dumb! However, I understand as I was one of those dumb people for a very long time. If you keep putting off hard conversations, you're undoubtedly going to regret it. Things may be fine for a while, but eventually everything will take a turn for the worse. The tension will build, the silence will grow, and the problems will multiply. Eventually, you'll be 20 years older and a hundred times more miserable—wondering *why the hell* you didn't speak up sooner!

****

"IF YOU'RE EAGER TO IMPROVE YOUR FAMILY LIFE, IT'S TIME TO LET GO OF THAT FEAR YOU'RE CLINGING ONTO."

****

If you're eager to improve your family life, it's time to let go of that fear you're clinging onto. Stop holding yourself back from initiating change because of what might happen if you do. It doesn't matter if you upset someone or create an uncomfortable situation—remember that bigger things are at stake here. You need to do what's best for your happiness and your future, and that means you need to be courageous. You need to act on how you feel rather than suppressing it. You need to chase after what you want instead of daydreaming about it. Desiring change doesn't make it happen; only *initiating* it does.

But what if you don't have time *right now* to reboot your family? You have a business to run, after all, so you're too busy to start something new. There's also no possible way that you can take off time from work, or stop working when you get home. You desperately want to improve your family, but it doesn't seem feasible right now. This excuse is all too common for entrepreneurs and business executives. We believe that we must work as much as possible in order to provide for our families. We fear that our companies will fail if we don't give them everything we've got. But if you truly care about your family and want to make things better, you can't make your life all about your career. In fact, you *can't* improve your family unless you make work less of a priority.

Before you can move on to the next step, understand that this needs to happen first. If you want your family members to be there for you, *you need be there for them.*

Even if you're working long and hard because you need to support your family financially, remember that financial support isn't the only support your family needs. In reality, our spouses and kids need *emotional* support more than anything else. Your family doesn't want your money, they want *you*. They want your guidance, your support, and most importantly—your love. If you're working long hours because money is tight at home, or because you want to make a surplus of it, remember that money isn't everything.

Maybe you're working long hours because it's just "who you are." You *enjoy* working, and you become stressed and restless when you aren't making progress toward something. You struggle to spend time with your family because relaxing feels like a waste of time. You just sit there contemplating how much work you could be getting done. You also truly believe that the more you work, the more money you will make—and that drives you to keep going.

If that sounds like you, realize that your desire to never stop working isn't healthy. People joke about being "workaholics," but being addicted to work is actually a very real condition. It's also a pretty serious one because it can have a dramatic impact on every area of your life. Along with dramatically affecting the quality of your work and relationships, it can harm your mental and physical wellbeing. If you stay obsessed with being productive, you will never attain peace of mind or fully enjoy the life you're living. If you don't slow down or take breaks, you will inevitably work yourself to death.

Why do you believe that working all the time is worth it? Does working all the time fulfill you completely? If your answer is no, then don't let work and productivity control your life. And realize that work isn't the only thing that's worth your time.

Maybe you're constantly working because it's your escape. You know that life isn't great at home, but you don't know how to confront the problem or change the path you're on. So you bury yourself in your work—using it as a temporary distraction. When you get home, you are disinterested and disengaged, which enables everyone else in the family to act the same way. You haven't had a genuine conversation with any of your family members in months, and you don't even know where your kids are most of the time. Worst of all, your spouse feels more like a roommate than a lover.

This is probably the most dangerous scenario of all. If you're allowing your life at home to remain stale and silent, you are fostering an environment of apathy and depression. You won't be the only one who is unfulfilled—everyone will feel this way. Nobody in your family will feel connected or even truly loved. I know many entrepreneurs who deal with this, and it truly breaks my heart. It mostly depresses me because I feel like it's the easiest situation to change! All they need to do is stop being cowards. If they stopped hiding in their work and started communicating with their families, they could enrich multiple lives.

Let me remind you and make this very clear: *all of these mindsets are unhealthy.* If you are more committed to your work than your family, you need to dig deep and identify exactly why that is. Then, if you want to protect your wellbeing and family, you need to change the way you think. Whenever you catch yourself in "work mode" when you shouldn't be, such as at home or during a family event, stop and just take a deep breath. Remind yourself why you can't prioritize work, and reflect on what really matters in life. This way, you can be in a healthy place before rebooting your family.

GET ALIGNED WITH YOUR SPOUSE

Once I felt confident that I was ready to reboot my family, I knew that the next thing I needed to do was talk to Rachel about it. No matter how badly I wanted to follow this roadmap, it couldn't happen unless I had her support. However, Rachel and I hadn't openly communicated about our relationship or family in a while, so I didn't feel like I could just spring my idea on her. I was certain that if I did, she would be totally caught off guard and wouldn't be as willing to participate.

In order to avoid this outcome, I wanted to get us more aligned first. If we both understood how we felt about our family's past, present, and future, it would be easier and more sensible to suggest the roadmap. But I knew that getting aligned would require talking to her about our relationship and family, which basically terrified me. I had no idea how to initiate this kind of conversation or what I should say. I considered what I could do to make the conversation go over more smoothly.

I started by asking myself, "How do I initiate hard conversations at work?" As I contemplated this, I eventually recalled a time when two of my employees struggled to get along. One of them really wanted to resolve the conflict, so they planned on openly talking to the other employee. However, months went by and the conversation never happened. I eventually asked the employee why they hadn't initiated the conversation yet, and she explained that there was never a right time or place to do so. She needed a safe and private place to initiate the conversation, which wasn't really available at our workplace at the time. Her answer made me realize how much our environments can affect our communication with others. I knew that if I wanted this conversation with Rachel to be as honest and effective as possible, it would need to take place in a safe and comfortable environment.

I would wait for the right time and place to talk to Rachel, but what exactly would I say? I wanted us to openly communicate and get more aligned, but I wasn't sure how to make this actually happen. Again, I considered my question from a business perspective. How was I able to get my employees more in sync and aligned? One of the answers was a no-brainer: team building activities. Every time my team and I have completed an activity together, I feel like we've grown closer and learned more about each other.

With that in mind, I began to consider if there was an activity that I could complete with Rachel. I researched and reviewed all sorts of ideas online, but I knew that none of them would produce the outcome I was aiming for. So, I decided to create my own. The activity I ended up creating was inspired by a successful activity that I've done with my Entrepreneurs' Organization group. My business partner Jason McDonald—who runs the Paris office for StringCan Interactive—also gave me feedback on my activity to make it more effective.

I ended up creating an activity called Talking About The Past Together, which consists of two worksheets. After I finished designing the worksheets, I waited patiently for the right moment to show Rachel. This moment ended up being on a Sunday morning after breakfast, when the kids were at my in-laws' house. We were both really positive and relaxed, and we had nowhere to be.

"Hey honey, so I created this activity that I think could really benefit us," I began. "It's meant to help us reflect on the past and get more aligned for the future. It sounds pretty easy and fun; can we try it out?" I asked. I kept my tone casual and my explanation simple so that she would be more willing to agree.

"Sure, if you think it's important," she replied. "But what exactly is it?" Now that she was basically onboard, I knew she deserved a more detailed explanation.

"It's two different worksheets," I replied. "The first one is about achievements."

We each write down three personal achievements from the past few months, three achievements that we admired in each other, and three achievements that we noticed in our family. Then we compare our answers and talk about them.

"The next worksheet is a reflection timeline of the past. We list out all of our major moments and milestones from the past year together, and then we rate them separately based on how much we loved or hated them. Then we compare our ratings and discuss where we align and differ."

"Hmm, that could be interesting … I really have no idea what you thought about this past year," Rachel replied. "Fine, let's try it out!"

We spent the next few hours completing the activity. And fortunately, it was just as beneficial as I had hoped. The achievements worksheet allowed us to focus on the positives first, which was exactly my intention. It also revealed what makes us most proud as individuals, spouses, and parents. Finally, it made us contemplate which achievements we want to accomplish in our future, which we talked about for five minutes or so.

The timeline activity was really eye-opening as well. It was really interesting to see which moments we rated similarly and to discuss why we both agreed. But without a doubt, the most intriguing part was when we found moments that we rated entirely differently. For example, Rachel rated our last cruise vacation as a positive eight while I only gave it a positive one.

"Why did you give the cruise such a low score?" Rachel asked.

"Well right before we left for the cruise, I had a huge problem come up at work. I was super stressed about it the whole time and couldn't stop thinking about it. That's why I bought the Wi-Fi service on the ship and tried to work a couple hours each day. But it was basically impossible to control what was happening in the office because I was so far away. That *really* frustrated me, so I didn't enjoy the vacation as much as I would have liked," I explained.

"Oh yeah, I remember you mentioning that something was going on. But if you couldn't control the problem from the ship, you should have just let it go instead of obsessing over it. There was nothing you could have done, so you should have just enjoyed the vacation. And we would have gotten to hang out with no-stress Jay for once!"

"I know, but I have a really hard time doing that. Half the time I don't even realize I'm off thinking about business, so how am I supposed to prevent it?"

"For starters, don't pay for Wi-Fi on cruise ships," she replied. "We both know it's ridiculously overpriced anyway." I smiled in agreement. "And in the future, when we can tell you're not really with us or stressing about business stuff, I'll point it out to you."

We continued to have these types of conversations as we compared our ratings. And let me tell you, being completely honest and transparent with each other felt *amazing*. I was finally able to get my thoughts and feelings off my chest, and I gained immense clarity into where Rachel and I currently stood. Even though some of the conversations were difficult and awkward, they were definitely worthwhile. By understanding each other's unique perspectives, thoughts and needs, we learned how to best get along and work together.

Once we had finally discussed everything on the timeline, we couldn't believe how much insight we gained from such a simple activity. We felt like we knew each other on a deeper level, which was really refreshing and exciting.

***

If you and your significant other haven't openly talked about your relationship or family in a long time, this is your next step. If you introduce the Family 2.0 Roadmap to your spouse before you two get aligned, they likely won't be as willing to participate. Even if they do agree to participate, the roadmap won't be as effective.

Think about it from a business perspective: You would never scale a company that didn't have solid foundation first. If you try to grow a company that isn't functioning well, it's a recipe for disaster. This is especially true when it comes to leadership. If the leaders on your team aren't aligned or committed, more problems will spread as the company continues to grow. These leaders won't be able to meet new company goals, motivate new team members, or overcome new challenges. Then, before you know it, your business' potential to succeed and grow is ruined.

****

"IF YOU WANT TO STRENGTHEN YOUR FAMILY, YOU MUST GET ALIGNED WITH YOUR SPOUSE FIRST."

****

If you want to strengthen your family, you must get aligned with your spouse first. Once you two are on the same page, they will likely want to improve your family just as much as you do. This way, when you suggest the Family 2.0 Roadmap, your partner will be more interested in pursuing it. You'll also begin to improve your relationship with each other, and you will work better together as you pursue the roadmap.

But let's make something clear. When I say "get aligned with your spouse," I don't mean that you need to reconcile all of your problems with each other. I also don't mean that you need to agree on everything or make any big changes. What I mean is that you should both discuss and understand how you feel about your current situation. This way, you can open the door to talking about your future and how to improve your family.

If you and your spouse haven't honestly talked about your relationship or family in a long time, I know this idea can sound intimidating. But remember: that's exactly why I created the Talking About The Past activity. This activity will help you and your partner initiate important conversations in a fun and positive way. Sure, you may still need to discuss some hard topics, but this activity will make those difficult conversations less challenging and negative. Why? Because the conversations will be surrounded by positive context.

Keep in mind that you will probably need about two to three hours to finish Talking About The Past. Ideally, if you have kids, reserve it for a time when the kids are not around. Also make sure that you and your spouse are in a relaxed state of mind before you begin.

When you're ready to bring up the activity, remember that your spouse will need some encouragement. Just be sure to stress that the activity is easy and beneficial so they won't have any reservations.

If they need some time to think about it, or they aren't willing to complete it right then and there, be willing to save the activity for a later time. Patience and persistence always pays off. One of my friends who went through this process was having a lot of communication issues with his wife. When he explained the Talking About The Past idea, she was not receptive. He did not give up and gave her some examples on the Achievement worksheet and it got her interested in giving it a shot.

Once you're ready to begin, start with Worksheet #1: Past Achievements. Print out two copies so that you two can complete it separately, and follow the instructions provided on the worksheet. If you're struggling to brainstorm achievements, remember that they don't need to be major or extraordinary. You can include small achievements too, such as doing taxes, planning a trip, losing two pounds, or finishing a project around the house. All that matters is that the accomplishments you choose make you truly happy and proud.

You'll notice that the worksheet says to choose achievements from the past three to six months. I chose this time period because I know it can be difficult to remember what happened more than six months ago (especially for us older folks). If you want to go back further than that, feel free to do so. Just make sure that you and your spouse both know what time period you're using.

After you've both completed your worksheets, take turns sharing what you wrote down and why. This will help you and your partner realize what's already going well in your lives. It will also create a safer, more vulnerable environment for having more difficult conversations.

Next, work together to create a list of all major events—both good and bad—that you two have experienced together over the last six to twelve months. Ideally, you want to create a list of 10-15 events. Again, feel free to change the time period if necessary.

If you have trouble remembering everything that happened in the past six to twelve months, don't panic (we definitely did too!). It all kind of blends together after a while, doesn't it? Thanks to today's digital age, you probably have more records of the past month than you even realize. For example, you can look through the photos you took on your smartphone or read through your social media posts. You can also browse through texts, look through calendar events, and review your bank statements. These records should certainly trigger some memories, and will even help you pinpoint exact dates.

After you've created this list, use Worksheet #2: Rating The Past. Print out two of them (one for yourself and one for your spouse) and follow the directions provided on the worksheet. Once your time-lines are complete, compare and discuss your results. Pay special attention to the areas where your ratings closely align and drasti-cally differ, and spend time evaluating them further. For example, if you both rated certain moments very low, discuss why you both didn't like these moments and if you can prevent them in the future. Or, if your spouse gave a moment a very high rating, but you rated it relatively low, find out why you rated them differently and what that tells you about each other. Be sure to listen—*really* listen—to your spouse so that you can better understand their perspective. Also, don't be afraid to ask questions.

When I suggested this activity to a friend, he brought up a concern. "Jay, my wife is under the impression that I loved traveling to Cancun last month. It was fun and all, but I actually really don't like traveling. She absolutely loves to travel though, so I just go along with it. If I give Cancun a really low rating, she's going to be really confused and upset when she sees my score. What do I do about that?"

You know what I told him? Deal with it! The whole purpose of the activity is to honestly communicate with your spouse, *especially* if you haven't been honest with each other in the past. If you've been lying to or deceiving your significant other, it needs to stop right now. It's impossible to strengthen a relationship that's built on lies, so you must be honest with each other before you can do so. Otherwise, your relationship will only continue to go downhill.

Let's consider my friend's situation further. If he continues to let his wife believe that he likes traveling, she's inevitably going to plan more trips with him that he doesn't actually want to go on. He'll also need to spend thousands of dollars and take more time off work to go on these trips that he doesn't care about. Over time, this will start to drive my friend crazy. He'll eventually become unhappy and resentful toward his wife, which will put stress on their relationship. Plus, he will need to continue concealing how much he dislikes traveling, which will become exhausting. Is that really how he wants to live?

When I explained this to my friend, he completely froze. I could tell that he had never thought about this way. "So, I just 'fess up?" he nervously asked.

"Yes," I replied. "Just explain that you aren't crazy about traveling, but you don't hate it either. That you're okay with going on trips occasionally, but you would love to find something else that you can both enjoy and do together." He thought that sounded easy enough, so he went for it. When we met up a few weeks later, I asked him how it went.

"She was definitely upset with me, but not for the reasons I was expecting," he explained. "Instead of being upset about the fact that I don't like traveling, she was really only mad that I didn't tell her sooner. I should have just been honest with her a long time ago. The best part was when we talked about our Cancun vacation in more detail, and there were actually a few parts about it I loved. Now when we go on a vacation we are going to set it up to do the things we both enjoy."

Learn from my friend's mistake, and be honest with your spouse starting right now. Lies and deceptions will only hinder your relationship and prevent you from being truly happy. Fortunately, this activity gives you the chance to come clean. And once you honestly open up about everything, you'll finally be able to strengthen your relationship and your family.

If you believe that you and your spouse are already really honest and aligned with each other, I applaud you two! I know that it takes a lot of courage and willpower to be transparent, so you definitely deserve some recognition. For you, the main benefit that you will gain from completing this activity is planning for the future. By identifying which past moments you and your spouse most liked and didn't like, you can better presume what future moments will make you two happiest. If you already know how each other feels about these past moments, focus on the small details. What small changes would make a big difference and improve each past event? If you find specific ways to make your experiences together even better, you can both be happier and more excited for the future.

For instance, maybe your family takes a California trip every summer. During the vacation, your family *always* wants to be on the beach. You like the beach, but after a couple days of sitting in the sand, you're pretty sick of it. On the third day of the trip, you would much rather go to the aquarium or a local restaurant instead of going to the beach again. However, you've never brought this up because it doesn't bother you that much. This activity is the perfect time to bring up even small details like this one. If you explain how happy this simple change would make you, your spouse will finally be aware of it and can actually make the change happen. As a result, you will enjoy vacation even more and be a happier person. Communicate what small changes would make a huge difference for you, and encourage your spouse to do the same. You'll be amazed about what you learn, and you'll be one step closer to improving your future together.

PITCH YOUR PLAN WISELY

After Rachel and I completed my activity together, the following weeks were noticeably more positive. Instead of forgetting that the other person was in the room or arguing about trivial things, we spent more quality time together and expressed how much we appreciated each other. We also talked more candidly about all sorts of topics, such as our family, personal aspirations, and creative ideas. One night, I explained to Rachel how happy I was that we were starting to connect better. I felt like we were having more meaningful conversations, and we better understood what we wanted out of life. She completely agreed with me.

"I think one of my ultimate goals for us is strengthening our family," I explained. "I know we don't hate each other or anything, but we don't always get along. The fighting and drama, especially with our kids,

****

"THE FIGHTING AND DRAMA, ESPECIALLY WITH OUR KIDS, MAKES ME WANT TO AVOID COMING HOME SOMETIMES."

****

makes me want to avoid coming home sometimes. Imagine if we all communicated better and really understood each other ... and if we agreed more on what we wanted our family to be like. I really think all of us would be so much happier."

I could see Rachel's eyes glistening as she thought about the idea. "Yeah, that would obviously be great! I'm not sure how we could realistically make that happen, though," she replied. "The girls are so young, and they're in that weird pre-teen place."

"Well, I actually have an idea. You know that annual goals planning process that I do with my StringCan team every year?" I asked her.

After she nodded, I said, "Well what if we did the same thing with our family? We could identify all the gaps that we want to overcome, and then create goals that will help us resolve those gaps and strengthen our family. Then we can meet together regularly to track our progress on each goal."

Rachel contemplated the idea for a minute before she responded. I could tell she was really thinking about it, but her facial expression didn't look promising.

FAMILY MEMBERS, NOT EMPLOYEES

"I don't know about that. It sounds like you're trying to treat our family like a business. We can't just treat our kids like they are employees," she said. "And I know that the process works really well for your team, but that doesn't mean it will work for us. I think it would be too complex for us, and it sounds like a lot of hard work."

As you can imagine, that wasn't the reaction I was hoping for. I felt like I had just gotten rejected, and I was disappointed that Rachel felt the way she did. I understood where she was coming from, but I definitely wasn't trying to treat our family like a business. I just knew that the framework of the process made sense, and it could benefit *any* type of group that wanted to communicate better and achieve great things.

Rachel was right about one thing though: the exact process that my employees went through certainly wouldn't work for my family. For example, I can't expect my kids to attend meetings or to "identify gaps." So instead of arguing with Rachel and trying to change her mind, I decided to let it go. I knew I had a better chance of gaining her support if I tried again later with a different approach.

Over the next few months, I began to brainstorm how I could make the process more family-friendly and less business-like. I read everything I could about families, talked with dozens of entrepreneurs, and even spoke with some psychiatrists. That's when I decided to take the framework of the process and create the Family 2.0 Roadmap. Although this roadmap would be similar to my annual business planning process, it would be executed in a different way. The steps and activities involved would be more appropriate and effective for my family.

Once the roadmap was ready, I couldn't wait to tell Rachel about it. I knew she would be more interested in this plan because it was tailored specifically to our family. But because I was blindsided by her rejection last time, I still needed to be careful with how I presented the roadmap. To ensure that it would go over smoothly, I waited for the right day and moment to bring it up. Eventually, the opportunity presented itself on a Saturday night when the girls were both at friends' houses.

Rachel was watching a show she recorded in the family room, so I grabbed a seat next to her on the couch. "Can I talk to you about something for a second?" I asked. She paused the show and looked up at me. "Of course, what's up?" she asked.

"I still really want to improve our family life, and I know that you do too. But I totally respect that you don't want to take our family through the process that I do with my StringCan team. I came up with a new idea, and I'd love to share with you. I think you'll like this idea a lot more than my last one," I explained.

"I'm listening," Rachel responded.

"Okay, well you were totally right when you said that the exact process my team goes through might not be effective for our family. I thought about that a lot, and it led me to create a new plan that will definitely benefit our family. It's similar to the annual goals process at StringCan, but it has a very unique, family-friendly spin on it. That's why we wouldn't even call it a process; it's more of a customized family roadmap now. There are no boring meetings or complex assignments involved. Instead, the roadmap includes a relaxing vacation, fun activities, and insightful conversations."

"Well this already sounds a lot better," Rachel replied. "How does it work?"

"The first part of this roadmap is the fun family vacation," I explained to Rachel, "but this vacation will be a little different than our typical ones. Along with having fun and doing all of the things we love, we'll spend time talking about the past year and planning out what we want to do next year. Our kids love crafty projects, so we'll use fun arts and craft activities to guide these conversations. Not only will these conversations empower us to have a great next year together, they will also help us open up to each other and grow closer together. Then, once the trip is over, we'll get together every month or so to talk about next steps for the goals and plans that we agreed to on the family retreat."

"Okay, that sounds like something we can possibly do," Rachel responded. "What are the activities you're referring to? What's all included in this?" Now that I knew she was open to the idea, I showed her the outline that I created for the roadmap.

At its most basic level, this is Family 2.0 Roadmap:

Part One: Communicate & Plan

1. Discuss what went well and didn't go well within the past year.

2. Consider and visualize what you want next year to look like.
3. Create goals that will make next year better.
4. Review, refine and align family goals.

Part Two: Pursue Change & Growth
1. Determine the next steps for every goal.
2. Regularly support and motivate each other to accomplish these goals.
3. Meet at least once a month to discuss progress on goals.

Now this roadmap might sound like a lot of steps to you, and you may be thinking, "My family would never be willing or able to do something like this!" But believe me, that's not true. In fact, the main reason I wrote this book was to ensure that *any family* could use this roadmap. This book offers invaluable insights, best practices, techniques and hands-on activities that you can use to successfully reboot your family. Once you finish reading this book, you and your family will have everything you need to follow this roadmap.

As I walked Rachel through each step on the outline, I explained what activities were involved. I also emphasized the benefits of each step so that she understood how the roadmap would strengthen our family life. For example, when I explained that the last step of Part One is "review, refine, and align family goals," I explained that this step will allow us to get all of our personal lives more in sync. It will also reveal how we can work together as a family to achieve the things we want, and how we can help each other be personally successful. This step will also enable us to balance and improve every area of our lives that truly matters to us. And of course, it will cultivate conversations that will bring us closer together.

By the time I finally finished going over each of the steps, I had mentioned dozens of benefits that the roadmap offers. However, if I were to summarize the benefits that this roadmap offers, it would be something like this:

- Experience more meaningful and effective communication
- Improve your relationship with everyone in your family
- Get along better as a family and effectively work together
- Spend more quality time together
- Empower everyone to live a more well-balanced life
- Make progress in every area of your life that matters
- Experience more peace and happiness
- Increase everyone's personal success and fulfillment

Presenting this roadmap and its benefits to Rachel was one of the best decisions of my life. It went over *a hundred times better* than I had hoped, and it just felt right for us. Rachel loved the idea so much that she got involved in helping me customize the roadmap even more. She had tons of great ideas she wanted to contribute, and I pretty much loved them all. Eventually, both of us were so excited about it that we could hardly wait to tell the kids.

***

Once you and your spouse are more aligned with each other, you should feel pretty comfortable about suggesting the roadmap. You should also feel better knowing that you won't be able to make the mistake that I did, which was proposing a business process instead of a customizable roadmap. As long as you are honest and respect-ful, this conversation will be one that you won't regret. Your spouse is bound to hear you out and become interested in pursuing the roadmap.

As you begin to explain this roadmap, here are some more communication dos and don'ts to keep in mind:

DO:

1. Find an appropriate time and place to talk. If you two rarely have free time together, plan a date night.
2. Verify that your spouse is in a good mental state by asking them how they are feeling.
3. Clarify that you would like his or her opinion on something.
4. Explain what's been bothering you in a non-accusatory manner, and then offer the potential solution (in other words, the Family 2.0 Roadmap!).
5. Paint a picture of what life would be like if you followed the roadmap.
6. Ask your spouse if they agree with how you're feeling, and if they would consider using the roadmap.
7. Ask your partner if they have any concerns.
8. Thank your significant other for sharing their thoughts.

DON'T:

1. "Gang up" on your spouse or point fingers. Don't start sentences with "You never ..." or "You always ..."
2. Use an authoritative tone of voice. Remember that you two are on the same team.
3. Force them to answer your questions or share their thoughts.
4. Get defensive.
5. Demand an immediate answer about the roadmap.
6. Get upset if they aren't interested in the idea at first.
7. End the conversation on a negative note.

Keep in mind that this conversation shouldn't be a really serious or negative one. All you need to do is tell your spouse that you want to go on a family trip that will strengthen your family. And this trip can happen anytime during the year.

If your partner disagrees with you or is hesitant for any reason, just be understanding and patient. It's not the end of the world; they probably just need time to process the idea. Eventually, I'm sure that your significant other will come around to the idea of rebooting your family. It took me a few different times and approaches to get Rachel on board, but it was certainly worth the effort in the end. Once your spouse agrees that they want to follow this roadmap, the next thing you'll need to do is get your kids involved.

GET YOUR KIDS TO "BUY-IN"

When Rachel and I were finally ready to talk to our daughters, we decided to plan a fun family dinner with Ella and Lexi. During dinner, I told the girls that we are going on a fun family trip to Pine, Arizona for four days. The four-day retreat can be done at any time during the year. We chose Pine because we decided to complete our family retreat in December and it usually snows there in December (and my daughters love the snow).

We showed them pictures of the cabin we would rent, and we talked about all the fun activities we could do while we were there. For instance, because there would be fresh snow outside our cabin, we told the girls we could build snowmen and drink hot chocolate. We also mentioned all of the delicious meals we could make, and named a few of the unique restaurants that would be nearby. I figured this would be a major selling point because everyone in my family is a foodie; we're all obsessed with eating unfamiliar foods and visiting new restaurants. Considering how excited Ella and Lexi got when I mentioned this, I was definitely right.

Eventually I said, "While we're on this trip, we're also going to plan out all of the fun stuff we want to do next year. Wouldn't that be cool?"

"Why do we need to plan out next year?" Lexi asked.

"So that we can make sure we get to do all the things we want!" I explained. "And if we plan it out together, everyone can have a say in what next year looks like."

They both thought it was a great idea. I couldn't believe how easy it was to get them on board! Now everyone was excited for the retreat, and I could finally stop worrying about getting buy-in. If your kids love vacations as much as mine do, I'm sure they will quickly buy in too. All you need to do is say you're going on a fun family trip that will involve planning out next year.

However, if your children are older or dread family time, you may need to use a more persuasive approach. To be more persuasive, treat this conversation like a business presentation to key stakeholders. When you're ready to present the retreat to your family, call for a family meeting when everyone is free. Then, as you would in a business presentation, first explain the problem in a rational manner.

Provide a few examples of obvious issues that your family is having. Maybe you fight too often, you don't acknowledge each other, or you don't respect each other's personal items. Whatever the bad habits may be, come prepared with specific examples. Don't forget to include yourself in these examples as well so it doesn't come across like you're just ganging up on everyone else. Explain how these actions negatively impact everyone mentally, emotionally, and/or physically. For example, if the issue is fighting, explain that fighting is a waste of everyone's time and it's physically bad for you because it raises your blood pressure.

Next, paint a picture of what life would be like if these issues were resolved. Explain that everyone would get along more often and being at home would be truly enjoyable. You would also trust each other more, and you would understand one another on a much deeper level. Your conversations with each other would be more transparent and meaningful—along with your relationships. As a result, you would all be empowered to live a happy, healthy life, and accomplish almost anything you desired.

Finally, offer the solution. Announce that you want to plan out next year together as a family. Explain that if you do this together, everyone can be happier moving forward. You don't need to provide all of the details as to how you will make this happen; just explain that it will involve a fun family trip. Your goal is to get your family excited for this upcoming trip, so find a way to appeal to their interests. For example, if your family love games, list some of the games you can play both outdoors and indoors. This way, everyone will get excited to participate.

CUSTOMIZING YOUR FAMILY ROADMAP

The roadmap that my family followed was mainly effective because I customized it to my family's unique habits, strengths, preferences and current issues. With that being said, the exact roadmap that your family follows doesn't need to be (and probably shouldn't be) the same as mine. Every family is different, so you may not get the best results if you follow my family's footsteps exactly. However, if you use what you know about your family to appropriately adjust this roadmap, you can ensure that you achieve the results you want.

ENVISION THE END RESULT

As an entrepreneur and businessperson, I understand the importance of having a clear and concise vision for where I want to go. For instance, because I have a vision for my business, I can make strategic decisions and stay on the right track. My business vision also reminds me that there is unfinished work to do and new goals to achieve, which pushes me and my team to work harder instead of simply coasting. For those reasons, my business vision is the driving force in StringCan's continual success and growth. And I think it would be nearly impossible to scale up my business if I didn't have a clear vision first.

With all of that in mind, I knew I couldn't reboot my family unless I had a clear vision for us first. If I didn't know where I wanted my family to end up, how could I ever get there? I started to imagine what my family would look like in five years (that is, if everything went the way I hoped and desired).

That's when I decided that more than anything, I didn't want my family to fight as much as we currently did. Instead of getting on each other's nerves and raising our voices, I wanted us to get along and communicate in a loving manner. And of course, I really just wanted all of us to stay true to who we really are as a family. I know that we share certain beliefs, morals and values—and those unique features are what make us the Feitlingers.

Before you start following this roadmap, take some time to decide what you desire most for your family. What exactly do you want to gain out of this experience? You say you want to align and strengthen your family, but what exactly does that look like for you? Because if you want to attain your most desirable results, you need to decide what those results are to begin with.

Keep in mind that this roadmap is only for one year, so you probably won't achieve this vision as soon as you complete the initial goals planning activities on your family trip. You will be *significantly closer* to achieving your ultimate family vision, and you will be much more aligned with it, but your vision will probably take at least a year to achieve. However, the main takeaway here is that if you and your family stay committed to this roadmap, your family vision will eventually become reality.

As you start to visualize your ideal family situation, focus on your family's core beliefs and values. Think about the type of culture and environment you want to create. What character traits is everyone exemplifying? How is everyone behaving? On Worksheet #3: Beliefs and Values, other questions are provided to help you clarify your family's core beliefs and values.

1. While you're answering these questions, keep these things in mind: **Stick to a one-year vision.** You will hopefully follow this roadmap every year, so focus solely on what you want to achieve this year.

2. **Keep your vision realistic.** If your vision is extremely un-likely or impossible to attain, then you will only be disap-pointed later on. While your vision should be ambitious and inspiring, it should also be practical and achievable.

3. **Ensure your vision isn't self-serving.** Try to create a family vision that your spouse and children will desire as much as you do. Because it is a *family* vision, everyone in your family should be eager to attain it.

Once you have a good idea of what your vision is for your family, fill out Worksheet #4: Describing Your Family Vision. The main point of this worksheet is to write down some of the keywords that illustrate your family vision. For instance, you might write words like respect, laughter, quality time, family dinners, confidence, and honesty. If you prefer, you can write out a paragraph or two that describes your vision, but don't feel pressured to perfectly string your words together.

Next, share your vision with your spouse. Explain why you chose the characteristics you did and ask for their insight. If they believe that your family vision is completely off-base, find out what they would change and why. Discuss this until you can both agree on what you desire most for your family. If you happen to strongly dis-agree with each other, find a way to compromise. For instance, you could each choose three values that matter most to you and focus on instilling all six into your family.

DETERMINE YOUR APPROACH

Once Rachel and I clarified what we wanted to gain out of this roadmap, I needed to decide how and where we were going to complete the goals planning activities in Part One. I knew that if I presented them as a series of "meetings," everyone would groan and quickly lose interest.

After considering my options, I decided that going on a retreat to a cabin for a few days would be the best way to complete Part One. My daughters get easily distracted, so I figured going somewhere quiet and away from home would help us stay focused on completing the goals planning activities. Plus, they love traveling and being in nature, so I knew that staying in a cabin would get them excited.

If your family likes traveling and you want to eliminate distractions, I highly recommend that you complete Part One as a family trip too. Plus, telling your family that you want to take them on a vacation is a great first step in improving your relationship with them. You don't necessarily need to stay in a cabin in the woods like my family did. If your family prefers hotels or a bed and breakfast experience, that's totally fine! You can also go to a more exciting place, like a city or a resort, but make sure the surrounding area won't take too much time away from the trip's activities.

Wherever you choose to go, just make sure it's somewhere that your spouse and kids can enjoy. Think about what kind of environments they are most comfortable in, as well as which ones drive them crazy. If you aren't sure, ask them! If everyone in your family is different, try to find a happy medium. For example, if one of your family members loves nature but another despises it, you could stay in a city that is located near a beautiful park. You can also give your family options for possible trips, and then choose the place that gets the most votes. But obviously, you and your spouse have the final say in where you end up going.

If you can't afford a family trip, or if your family can't get time off together, there are other ways you can complete the activities in Part One. For example, you can break the activities up into sessions and complete each one at a weekly family breakfast, lunch or dinner. You could also plan a more affordable camping trip or staycation, and complete the activities there. In short, just find a creative way to get your family together for good chunks of time. Think about each of your schedules and availability. When will everyone have time for "meetings?"

As you consider how you will complete Part One, don't forget to keep in mind how much time they will require. For my family, four days was the perfect amount of time. It never felt like we were rushing through the activities or overextending ourselves, and we were able to have important, meaningful conversations every day. We also had plenty of free time to have fun and relax, which gave us opportunities to enjoy our vacation instead of just constantly working. I suggest that your family dedicates approximately four days to Part One too.

Nonetheless, some families may be able to complete Part One in less than four days. Especially if most of your family members are older and everyone gets along pretty well, you can probably complete Part One in just one day. However, it's critical that you don't rush through any of the activities or overexert yourselves, because doing so won't allow you to get the most out of this experience.

To better determine how much time you should dedicate to Part One, use the following guidelines:

The extended version (3-5 days) is best for:

- Children ages seven to 13
- Shy or quiet family members
- Families with more than four members
- Families who rarely communicate
- Discussing serious problems or topics
- Discussing dozens of problems or topics

The condensed version (one day) is best for:

- Children ages 13+
- Families with less than four members
- Families who communicate regularly
- Outgoing, talkative family members
- Families who are in touch with their emotions
- Families with minimal or minor issues

PICK YOUR FAMILY CATEGORIES

During the retreat, I knew my family and I would have plenty of time for important conversations and family bonding time. But once we got back to real life, keeping our bond strong and making time for everyone would be extremely challenging. Various factors like work tasks, school assignments, friends or colleagues would distract us and consume most of our time. As a result, we would probably focus less on our family goals and eventually lose all the progress we made.

For that reason, I knew that the Family 2.0 strategy couldn't be solely focused on improving our family. Although family is important, I didn't want or expect us to sacrifice other priorities like our health, friends or career goals to make our family better. That would be unfair and unrealistic, especially because these areas of our lives matter just as much as our family does. During the retreat, I wanted us all to find out how to balance all of the different areas and priorities within our lives. This way, we could ensure that everything that mattered to us got the attention it deserved—including our family.

In order for us to accomplish this task, I would first need to pinpoint all of the major areas and priorities within our lives. This way, we could make sure we factored everything that mattered into the equation. I asked Rachel to help me with this task so that I could get another person's perspective on the matter.

Fortunately, because we had already envisioned what we wanted for our family, this task wasn't difficult. We knew what our values and beliefs were, and we understood what success looked like for each of us. Using that information, we were able to brainstorm most of our major life priorities. Once we had a list of 10, we felt pretty confident that we had identified all of the main areas within our lives. If we dedicated time to each of these areas and balanced them all, we believed that we could be truly happy and successful. We ended up calling these various areas our family categories.

Our family categories include:

- Personal Development/Learning (e.g. gaining new skills or hobbies)
- Family (e.g. spending quality time together, supporting each other)
- Money (i.e. earning, saving and spending money)

- Pleasure (e.g. going on vacation, reading, eating, doing fun activities)
- Relationships (i.e. improving relationships with specific family members or friends)
- School/Career (e.g. getting good grades, following certain career paths)
- Health (e.g. exercising, losing weight, eating well)
- Social (e.g. attending social events)
- Public Service/Community (e.g. donating, volunteering)
- Spirituality (e.g. going to temple or church, meditation, journaling, praying)

***

Before you go on the retreat, consider your family's priorities and create your family categories. This way, you can figure out how to best balance them all while you're on your family trip. Some categories that should definitely be on your list are family, friends, health, pleasure and school/career. The others are completely up to you.

To successfully determine your family' categories, complete Worksheet #5: Creating Your Family Categories.

- Where do we (and should we) invest most of our time?
- What areas of our lives do we care about most?
- What defines us as a family, and as individuals?
- What priorities must be met in order for our family to live a well-balanced life?
- What priorities must be met in order for our family to be happy, healthy and successful?

As you answer these questions, create a list of all the categories you come up with. You should have at least five categories and no more than 10. If you have over 10, see if any categories on the list can be combined (or cross out a few that don't really belong). Otherwise, the roadmap will be more time-consuming and difficult for you. Once you have 5-10 categories, review them with your spouse to ensure that they agree. Or, if you prefer, get your partner involved earlier on like I did. Once we were done with our categories, we created a hub and spoke wheel poster that would be visual for our kids to convey the important categories for our family. You can present the list in a way that works best for your family.

CREATE YOUR FAMILY TIMELINE

One night when Rachel and I were talking about the retreat, we were discussing what we wanted the very first activity to be. I reminded her about the worksheets we did together, and I proposed that we complete them again as a family. I felt like the worksheets made it a hundred times easier to honestly communicate and initiate hard conversations, so I thought the girls could benefit from them too. Plus, even though Rachel and I already did them together, completing them again as a family could be a totally different experience. If the kids were involved, the events we put on the timeline and the conversations we initiated would likely change.

Rachel agreed with me, but she didn't think the Achievements worksheet was necessary. Our family is pretty positive for the most part, so we believed the Achievements worksheet wouldn't provide much value. She also felt that completing two worksheets would be too much work to start with, which I totally understood. We decided to only focus on Rating the Past.

However, we realized that we would need to modify the first step on the Rating the Past worksheet. If all four of us brainstormed a list of past events together, the list could end up being really long and overwhelming. The activity would be really tedious as a result, and we may not even get to talk about topics that really mattered. To avoid this, Rachel and I decided to prepare the list of timeline events ahead of time but we removed the rating scale to allow our children the chance to share how they felt about the past events.

As we reviewed our calendars and photos, we chose events that we believed would generate the most insightful and beneficial conversations. For example, Rachel and I really wanted to talk about the fights we've been having, so we included a time when all of us got into a heated argument at a restaurant. We also included a lot of positive moments like family vacations, birthday parties, big projects and new school years. We figured if we all talked about both our worst and best moments, we could determine what works and doesn't work for us. Fill out Worksheet #6: Family Timeline to help complete this process.

By the end of it, we had a list of 15 events from the past year. It felt great knowing that we had saved ourselves a lot of time and trouble on the retreat, but we felt like something was still missing. The list of events looked pretty long and uninteresting, and the worksheets I created were pretty plain. We didn't want this to feel like a boring homework assignment; we wanted it to be a fun activity!

In hopes of getting the girls more excited about it, we turned our list of events into a visual family timeline. We used a poster board, markers and colorful sticky notes to map out each event on a solid line. Once it was done, we were both really happy that we put in the extra effort. It was definitely more appealing than a bulleted list of events, and it was exciting to have our own family timeline. We just knew the girls would love it.

Before the retreat begins, I definitely recommend that you create your family timeline. Doing so will make it easier for everyone to complete the Rating the Past worksheet. Even if you don't want to complete the worksheets, presenting and reviewing your family timeline will help you facilitate important conversations. Plus, it's just a fun and creative way to kick off the retreat.

Creating your family timeline doesn't need to be challenging either. Just pick 10-20 past events that you and your spouse want to discuss as a family, and create some type of visual for it. You can use a poster board like we did, or you can create it digitally if you prefer. However, keep in mind that everyone needs to be able to see it, so the format should be easily presentable. If you end up doing this digitally, I suggest you print out one color copy for each family member so they can refer to it throughout the day. Feel free to include pictures, icons, stickers or any other fun elements to make it more visually appealing. Remember that this isn't a business project—it's a creative activity that represents your family's past year together.

GET THE RIGHT RESOURCES

When I complete the annual goals planning process with StringCan, we use a lot of digital tools. However, I really didn't expect or even want my family to use these digital tools during the retreat. In fact, I wanted to minimize the use of technology as much as possible on this trip because I know that everyone in my family is clearly addicted to it. If we were on our phones and laptops on this trip, I knew that we would be constantly distracted and hardly talking to each other. By restricting the use of technology on this trip, everyone would be more focused and engaged. It would also prove that we don't need technology to enjoy the vacation or spending time together.

Instead of using technology and digital tools during the retreat, I decided that we would use arts and crafts. I knew we could complete all the activities with art supplies, so I believed this was the perfect alternative. Plus, we're a very visual and creative family, so it matched our personalities.

Because I know how distracting and addicting technology can be, I highly suggest that you avoid using technology on your trip too. View this trip as an opportunity for a technology cleanse—a chance to prove that you and your family don't need technology to be happy. Especially if technology is currently preventing your family from interacting, restricting it on this trip is one of the best decisions you can make. This way, your family can learn how to communicate and co-exist without it.

If you decide to utilize the activities explained in this book, and you don't want to use technology to complete them, review Worksheet #7: Retreat Supplies such as poster boards, relevant magazines, scissors, and glue sticks.

Although I recommend foregoing technology during this process, I understand that some adults and children are completely unwilling to give it up. Also, some families are very tech-savvy and prefer to use digital tools whenever possible. Or maybe your family just really hates arts and crafts and isn't very creative. If any of these scenarios are true for your family, it's okay to use digital tools. Just stick to basic tools like Google Slides and Notes so that you don't make the retreat more techy that it needs to be.

GET IN THE RIGHT MINDSET

After you've completed all of the tasks previously mentioned, there's just one last thing you need to do before the retreat begins: get yourself in the right mindset. Yes, you've already committed yourself to rebooting your family, and you already know what you want to get out of the retreat, but you haven't yet agreed to maintain the ideal mindset. And if you want your family retreat to be successful, being in the right mindset will be essential. Otherwise, you will hold yourself and your family back.

As an entrepreneur or businessperson, you've probably experienced this. In order to scale a business, you must embrace a growth mindset and be agile in your thinking. Because if you are open-minded and flexible, you will be much more likely to initiate necessary change and adapt well to new business pressures. This means you can more successfully scale your business.

****

"IF YOU'RE WILLING TO ADAPT AND GROW, YOU CAN MORE SUCCESSFULLY IMPROVE YOUR CURRENT FAMILY SITUATION."

****

Well, the same philosophy applies to improving your family! If you're willing to adapt and grow, you can more successfully improve your current family situation. But that's not the only mindset that you should commit to while on this retreat. If you want this trip to be as successful as possible, you should maintain a positive and present state of mind too.

To get yourself in the ideal mindset for this retreat, here are some things you can do:

1. **Leave the business behind.** You're away from the office and not around your employees, so embrace the fact that you don't need to be a boss or businessperson on this trip. Instead, you can dedicate your attention to being a loving spouse and parent.

2. **Stay away from technology.** Another reason why we recommend limiting electronics on this trip is to help you get away from it yourself. Checking your email every five minutes is the last thing you want to do when you're trying to focus on your family.

3. **Clear your mind.** If you can't stop thinking about work, write down all of your thoughts and then *let them go*. If your mind still won't stop racing, take some deep breaths or consider meditating.

4. **Be present.** Stop thinking about the past or the future. Instead, just be in the moment. Whenever a new thought crosses your mind, just let it go or write it down instead of getting lost in it.

5. **Be happy.** Your attitude is contagious. Smiling and thinking happy thoughts will make you and those around you feel happier.

6. **Embrace your inner child.** Don't look down on your kids for acting childish or weird—instead, join them! Be silly, dance around, and don't care what anyone else thinks. Rediscover

the bliss of being a child who is free from the weight of the world.

7. **Feel the love.** Can you remember when you first fell in love with your spouse? Can you relive the day that your children were born? Embrace those moments once again and let them fill your heart with love.

8. **Focus on what you want.** The law of attraction is a powerful tool. Focus on what you want to happen on this trip rather than what you don't want to happen. This way, you'll be much more likely to attain it.

These tips may seem obvious, but take some time to consciously commit to each of them prior to your first family trip. I also suggest that you look these over every morning on the trip and any time when you know you aren't in the best mood. If you maintain the right state of mind on this trip, everyone else will be inspired to do the same. Also, if you show that you have faith in your family's ability to change, everyone else will have more faith too. As a result, all of your family members will have a better experience and be more willing to change.

DAY ONE:
THE JOURNEY BEGINS

DAY ONE: STEP-BY-STEP

1. Travel to your destination
2. Get settled in and relax
3. Do a fun family activity together (e.g. cooking dinner)
4. Go over the plans and goals for the retreat
5. Review the basic guidelines for the retreat
6. Give everyone their journals and provide time to write
7. Talk privately with your spouse

THE IDEAL FAMILY ROAD TRIP

Let's face it—nobody loves being stuck in a car with their family for an extended amount of time. Especially if you have young children or if your family doesn't get along, road trips can really test your patience and push you to your limits. In fact, if your family road trips are anything like ours, I'm sure you've had moments when you almost completely lost it.

When we go on family road trips, my daughters somehow always find ways to drive Rachel and me crazy. They bicker with each other, complain about the drive, beg us to pull over for potty breaks every thirty minutes, etc. They are also super chatty and energetic, so they often get unreasonably rowdy or antsy like most children do.

Even though these behaviors really annoy Rachel, and me we usually just deal with them because that's just how kids are, right? But we were committed to strengthening our family on this retreat, so we knew this road trip needed to be different. Plus, Rachel and I shouldn't have to be miserable on every family road trip just because we have kids. After all, there must be ways to make family road trips enjoyable for everyone. Once I had this realization, I started to brainstorm what these solutions could be. How could I help my daughters calm down and behave on road trips?

When I thought about it, I realized that my team at StringCan is a pretty rambunctious group too. In fact, sometimes they're so rowdy that being at work is more distracting than being at home with my kids! It keeps work enjoyable and entertaining, so I usually don't mind. But every once in awhile, it definitely becomes too distracting. When it started happening on a regular basis, I decided I needed to say something during one of our team meetings.

"Guys, remember that one day when you were blasting music and dancing around the office? Or that time when we spent hours acting out fake Shark Tank episodes?" They all chuckled and nodded.

"I love that we have fun here, but sometimes I think we just need to take a deep breath and calm down. We're starting to get too carried away for too long, and it really doesn't benefit us. It honestly wastes our time and energy, and it distracts us from focusing on what really matters. I would like us to find a way to minimize the rowdiness. If we can do that, we will be a lot more productive and successful. Would you guys agree?" After they all meekly nodded and apologized, we started brainstorming ways to control our craziness.

Eventually, we came up with an effective solution. We decided that if we ever notice somebody on the team is getting too rowdy or carried away, we speak up and ask them to chill out. We also encourage them to take a few deep breaths to help them calm down.

After I had this conversation with my team, I was incredibly relieved that I said something about the rowdiness. If I avoided bringing it up and I let my frustrations build, things could have gotten much worse. For instance, I probably would have blown up on the next person who veered off track at work. Then my employees would lose respect for me and develop a negative perception of me, which would inevitably cause new problems. But fortunately, I was transparent and honest with my employees instead. Everyone was much more responsive and apologetic as a result, and we were even able to come up with an effective solution. I decided that I should probably use this approach with my family. However, my kids are not my employees, so I needed to customize this solution for my family.

After we loaded up the car and got everyone situated for the long car ride, I got in driver's seat and turned around to look at Ella and Lexi.

"Okay, so we're ready to hit the road! But before we do, I just want to say a couple things. Girls, can you recall our past family road trips? Do you remember how antsy and cranky we usually get?" They both nodded. "Well I would like us to avoid those feelings this time. Instead, I would like us all to stay positive, calm and respectful. This way, the journey to the cabin will be a lot of fun and we will get there faster!"

"Okay!" They both replied. I knew it couldn't be that simple though, so I kept going.

"Now there will probably be moments when being happy is really hard, especially if we're upset or frustrated. So when something is bothering us, let's speak up and communicate how we're feeling instead of getting angry or yelling at one another. Can we try to do that?"

"Yeah!" They both replied.

About an hour into the road trip, I started to wonder if we would really have any troubles getting along. The girls ended up watching the rest of a movie and Rachel fell asleep, so the first hour was pretty painless. But eventually the movie ended and Rachel woke up, and suddenly everyone was a *lot* more energetic and talkative.

At one point, Lexi and Ella were talking about a movie they recently saw. They were acting out scenes, laughing like crazy, and recalling certain events. The conversation didn't bother me at all, but they were talking *unreasonably* loudly! I knew they were probably just excited and unaware that they were shouting, but they were really aggravating and distracting me. I realized that this was a perfect moment to speak up about how I was feeling, but I wasn't sure what I should say. Usually I yell something rude or aggressive, but that's exactly what we were trying to avoid doing on this car ride. What could I say instead?

After I thought about it for a minute, I blurted out, "BACON!" Everyone in the car instantly stopped what they were doing and stared at me.

"You are so weird. Why did you just yell bacon?" Rachel asked, looking completely puzzled. The girls started laughing and gave me the "I have the strangest dad ever" look.

"Well I wanted to speak up about something that's bothering me, but I didn't want to be rude about it," I explained.

"Alright then ... I guess being weird is better than being rude," Rachel jokingly reasoned. "So, what's wrong?"

"I'm just having a hard time focusing on the road because Ella and Lexi are talking really loudly. Would you girls mind taking it down a few decibels?" I said.

"Sure! I want to my play a game on my iPad anyway," Lexi replied.

"Me too!" Ella added.

And just like that, it was silent. I couldn't even believe it ... It was such a silly and simple technique, but it actually worked! And for the first time in a long time, I did not yell at them and get everyone in a bad mood.

Later on the drive, Rachel ended up using my bacon trick too. She didn't say it because of Lexi or Ella, though. She actually said it because my slow driving was making her anxious. Normally I get annoyed or defensive when she tells me to speed up, but because she yelled, "Bacon!" I just laughed and agreed to go faster instead.

Expressing how we felt during the drive and agreeing on solutions wasn't always easy, but we got better at it over time. For example, one time after I yelled out, "Bacon!" I explained that the music the girls were playing was making me unreasonably irritable. I love music but after too many Bieber and Swift songs, I felt like my blood pressure was rising with every new song that came on. Once I explained to Ella and Lexi that I needed silence, they threw a fit.

"You can't just turn off the music, Daddy! Silence is boring!" Lexi exclaimed.

"But this music is almost unbearable for me," I said.

"We really want to hear the next song, though," Ella replied. "Please don't make us turn it off!"

"What if we just change it to something we can both tolerate? Isn't that a fair compromise?" I pleaded.

"Fine..." they both mumbled. "But we want to listen to the next song first!" I *really* didn't want to listen to another kid's song, but I knew I needed to suck it up. If I was asking them to compromise, then I needed to be willing to compromise too. Even though the next song drove me crazier than all the others, I let it play. Then we listened to another pop artist that I could actually tolerate.

When you're traveling to your destination, you can use this technique to help your family get along better too. It should hopefully help you minimize fights and unruly behavior while en route. As a result, you will *finally* be able to enjoy family road trips—and traveling with your family in general.

If you don't think my technique will work for your family, there are several other things you can do to improve your family road trips. Car games are a great example. In addition to helping everyone work together and get along, car games make the time go by faster. They also help everyone embrace their childlike side and think more creatively, which will make the retreat go more smoothly. Plus, they are just plain fun!

Here are some classic examples of car games you can play:

- **20 Questions.** Player One chooses a person, place or thing. Then everyone else takes turns asking questions that can be answered with a simple "yes" or "no." Once your 20 questions are up, you have three more tries to guess what the object is. The person who guesses it first wins! If nobody guesses it, Player One wins.

- **Tell a Story.** Start off a narrative by saying something like "One time when I was driving to my friend's house ..." and then have the family member next to you contribute something to the story. Let everyone take turns contributing until you have a complete narrative—or until the narrative gets too ridiculous as it often does in my family.

- **Endless Questions.** Ask a question, but only allow the family member closest to you to respond with another question. Keep going around the car so that everyone can play. When someone fails to respond with a question, they are out. When only one player is left, they are the winner and the game is over.

- **Categories.** Choose a category that everyone is familiar with, such as types of cereal or Disney movies. Then take turns naming off one thing in that category, and don't let anyone pass their turn. When someone gives an answer that was already said or makes no sense, or if they can't think of anything to say, they are out. The last one standing is the winner.

If you haven't played these games on family road trips in the past, I suggest that you give it a try. Even if your children are older, they will still enjoy these games and find them entertaining. After all, you're never too old to play games. Also, keep in mind that there are dozens of other car games out there. If you don't think your family will like the ones I've listed here, research some other games and choose the ones that fit your family's personality best.

As a final tip for improving your family road trips, be sure to bring along things that will keep everyone busy. For example, bring magazines, headphones, snacks, toys, stuffed animals, or anything else that your kids often play with. If everyone has something to do during the car ride, they will be a lot less likely to get agitated or upset.

I know we said to limit the use of technology on the retreat, but the road trip to get there is an exception. You won't be trying to have in-depth conversations in the car, so you don't need everyone to be present and engaged just yet. Plus, not allowing technology on a long car ride will seem like a cruel and unusual punishment. Let your family use technology as much as they want in the car, but let them know that their time with technology ends once the retreat begins.

AN UNSETTLING ARRIVAL

When we finally arrived to our cabin in Pine, Rachel and I took a sigh of relief. The road trip to the cabin was officially a success, which meant nobody wanted to kill each other. In fact, everyone was still in a relatively positive mood after two hours of driving. We were incredibly thankful that the retreat was off to a great start, and we couldn't wait to see how the rest of the trip would go.

Once we parked the car, the girls all jumped out and raced up to the front door of the cabin. As soon as I unlocked it and we stepped inside, we immediately "oohed" and "aahed" over how spacious and beautiful it was. The cabin was definitely more astonishing than any of us were expecting, so it was a very pleasant surprise.

I knew the cabin had a loft with multiple beds, so I told Ella and Lexi to go explore and choose their beds and start unpacking. Considering that they behaved so well on the long car ride, I figured that they deserved to pick their own beds. As soon as I gave them permission to do so, they raced up the stairs and started exploring the loft. Even though Rachel and I stayed downstairs, we could hear their eager footsteps and excited squeals. But not even five minutes later, the sounds of rushed footsteps and joyous cries stopped. Then, out of nowhere, they started screaming furiously at each other.

"I don't care what you say, Lexi! This bed is mine!" Ella demanded.

"You always get what you want Ella, it's not fair! I'm the oldest, so I get to pick my bed first. And I want the bigger one!" Lexi yelled.

Once Rachel and I realized that they were fighting, we just stared at each other in disappointment. What was I thinking? This retreat was going to be a disaster! No matter how much we teach our daughters about behaving and getting along, they will never stop fighting. This moment truly shattered all of my hope and optimism. Just like that, I was now nervous and doubtful about the entire retreat and roadmap.

"This is exactly what shouldn't happen on this trip!" I moaned. "What do we do? Should I just go up there and tell them to cut it out?" I asked Rachel.

"No, let's try a different approach this time," Rachel replied. "If changing our approach worked in the car, maybe it can work in the cabin too. It's worth a shot at least, right?"

I knew Rachel was right, especially because this logic is true in the world of business. If you aren't getting the results you want from your business or your team, you need to change your approach. Otherwise, you're just doing the same thing over and over again and expecting different results, which is just silly! I started brainstorming how we could resolve the fighting differently this time around. Instead of yelling at Ella and Lexi to stop like I usually do, maybe I could try using a more peaceful approach.

"How about we just go up there and calmly ask them what's going on? Then, we can discuss a rational solution together?" I suggested. Rachel loved the idea.

We headed upstairs and followed the sound of high-pitched screams. As we approached the girls, we remained completely silent. They both stopped yelling when they first saw us, but then they tried to pull us into the argument.

"Dad, I really want this bed but Lexi won't give it to me! She's also being really mean!" Ella declared.

"Stop acting like it's all my fault, Ella! You were mean to me first, but I'm not being a big baby like you are," Lexi exclaimed.

That's when Ella started crying, which is a pretty common occurrence in these situations. It's always disheartening to see her cry, but I know that Rachel and I can't always take Ella's side just because she gets upset more easily. It's really not fair to Lexi. I tried to remove my emotions from the situation and resisted consoling Ella.

"Listen girls, I don't care who was mean first. I just want to know why you started fighting in the first place," I calmly stated.

"This is the best bed in the whole cabin, so we both want it," Ella explained.

"But Dad, I said I wanted it first! Ella didn't say she wanted it until after I said that I wanted it," Lexi added.

"But I wanted it first! I just hadn't said it out loud yet!" Ella replied.

Wow, why did I let them choose their own beds?! That was clearly a mistake. Now I somehow had to rationally resolve this fight, and I really wasn't sure how I was going to do that. I looked over at Rachel in distress. Hopefully, she had an idea to share.

"What if you each got this bed, but on different nights? I think that would be a fair compromise," Rachel suggested. Whew, she is really brilliant sometimes!

"I agree, that does seem like a fair solution," I concurred.

"But, who would get the bed first?" Lexi asked.

"Let's just flip a coin!" I said, as I pulled out a quarter from my pocket. "Heads means that Lexi gets the bed first, and tails means that Ella gets the bed first." I tossed up the coin before anyone could argue, and it landed heads up. Lexi cheered with joy, while Ella got really depressed and teary-eyed.

As much as I wanted to console Ella and give her the room first instead, I knew that I needed to stop favoring her as much as I do. Otherwise, she would never learn that she can't always get what she wants, which could lead to bigger issues later on. Instead of changing the outcome of the coin toss or giving Ella all of my attention, I remained fair and logical.

"Lexi, the bed is yours for tonight," I confirmed. "But Ella, that shouldn't make you sad! The bed will be yours tomorrow, so now you have something to look forward to. And at least Lexi didn't get the bed for every night," I pointed out. Ella was still sad, but I could tell that my comments cheered her up a little.

Before Rachel and I left the loft, I spoke up again. "Girls, I have one last thing to say. And I want you to take this seriously," I began. Once it was clear that I had their full attention, I continued.

"The fighting between you two and all of us really needs to get under control. So while we're on this retreat, I would like us all to try a little bit harder to get along. If you disagree about something, don't just start yelling at one another! That will only cause more problems and can even lead to punishments. Instead of fighting, just find a way to compromise. For example, if you're arguing over things like toys or beds, consider sharing them or taking turns. That way, everyone wins and nobody's feelings get hurt. Do we think we can do that?" I asked.

"Yeah, we can try," Lexi said.

"Okay, I like that!" Ella concurred.

After I thanked them, Rachel and I headed back downstairs. We were both amazed and excited that our new plan had actually worked. I felt ridiculous for becoming hopeless earlier; we clearly still had a chance to strengthen our family. At that moment, I told myself I wouldn't jump to any more conclusions while on this trip. If I lost hope for my family or became doubtful about this roadmap, I wouldn't be able to help us overcome the hurdles we encountered. And that's supposed to be the whole point of this roadmap! Plus, if I gave up, what kind of message would that send to my wife and kids? That I no longer care to strengthen our family? I couldn't do that, especially because it would never be true. I decided that I would stay in the right mindset throughout this trip and roadmap no matter what happened. If I committed myself to being flexible, loving and confident, I could help my family get through any problem or complication that came our way.

For the same reasons, I urge you to avoid becoming hopeless or discouraged while on your trip. Even if things get ugly or don't go according to plan, don't assume that the retreat is suddenly a disaster. Instead, view it as a learning opportunity. Test out different techniques, approaches or compromises to see what works best. If you're innovative, agile and work through family problems together as a team, you will be amazed at what you're able to accomplish.

START WITH SOMETHING SIMPLE

After being stuck in a car together and fighting over bedrooms, I figured we all needed some time to unwind and relax. After we finished unpacking the car, we took some time to get settled in and cleaned up. About an hour later, everyone was ready and eager to make the dinner we planned.

We all gathered in the kitchen and tracked down all of the ingredients and supplies we needed. Once we had everything, Rachel prepared the main course while I helped Ella and Lexi make side dishes. We played music, danced around, and took as much time as we needed.

Without a doubt, making dinner together was the perfect way to kick off the retreat. It allowed us to practice working together as a team before starting any of the activities. Making dinner together also gave us the opportunity to let loose, have fun and spend quality time together before getting into anything serious. As a result, all of us were getting along well and thoroughly enjoying ourselves once it was finally time to eat.

Hopefully, after your family arrives and gets settled in, you can make dinner together like my family did too. But if that's not possible where you're staying, find another activity that your family can enjoy together. This activity will largely depend on what time of the day it is when you arrive and what your family likes to do. Choose an activity that is practical for your circumstances, but make sure that it's something everyone in your family can enjoy (or at the very least, tolerate). Most importantly, choose an activity that will involve everyone.

Ideas for Fun Family Activities

- Eating at a unique restaurant
- Playing board games (e.g. Scrabble, Monopoly)
- Playing outside games (e.g. Hide and Seek, Capture the Flag)
- Going on a walk or hike
- Creating and then going on a scavenger hunt
- Swimming or fishing
- Bowling
- Playing laser tag
- Roller skating or ice skating
- Getting ice cream or frozen yogurt
- Building a blanket fort
- Having an outdoor fire and making s'mores

Once you start your family activity, pay attention to how everyone is acting. Are all of your family members having fun and participating? If you notice that anyone isn't behaving right or seems unhappy, don't be afraid to say something. This retreat is all about confronting and resolving family issues, so take advantage of moments like these instead of overlooking them.

You can simply ask the disgruntled family member, "What would you rather do instead?" If they reply with a logical answer, find a way to resolve the problem. For instance, maybe they don't feel good or they're really tired. If that's the case, you could find a new activity that requires less energy or you could let them go lay down for a few minutes. If it's a more complicated situation, take however much time you need to listen and talk through possible solutions (more on this later).

If your family member doesn't have a legitimate reason for their behavior, tell them how it's making you feel. For example, you might explain that their attitude is preventing everyone from being happy and is personally upsetting you. Then politely ask them to change their attitude so that everyone—including themselves—can enjoy the trip more. If they are stubborn and unwilling to change, tell them that they are excluded from the activity until they change their attitude. After you say this, walk away and avoid giving them any attention. If you give them some time alone to settle down and self-reflect, there's a good chance that they will change their attitude.

****

"PEOPLE DON'T ALWAYS ADMIT WHEN SOMETHING IS WRONG, BUT THEIR ACTIONS WILL SURELY SHOW IT."

****

Paying close attention to how your family members are acting and feeling will be critical throughout the entire retreat. People don't always admit when something is wrong, but their actions will surely show it. By staying aware of how your family members are acting, you can more effectively tell when something is wrong and unveil problems that would otherwise go unnoticed. Then you can find ways to resolve these problems so that your family members no longer display these negative behaviors.

THE DINNER CONVERSATION

About halfway through dinner, Rachel and I explained to Ella and Lexi what the plans were for the rest of the trip. "Okay girls, so as I mentioned before, the main reason we're on this trip is to plan out a really fun next year as a family," I started. "To accomplish this goal, we're going to complete a specific activity each day. Once we've completed the main activity for the day, we can do some of the really fun things we talked about."

"For instance, after breakfast tomorrow, we're going to talk about what we liked and didn't like about this past year. We'll each create our own reflection board to display our thoughts, and then we'll each get a chance to present our boards. Then we'll go play outside, build snowmen, drink hot chocolate and enjoy dinner. Doesn't that sound like fun?!" I excitedly asked them.

"Yeah!" Ella and Lexi cheered. "But what is a reflection board?" asked Lexi. I explained to them that the reflection board is a chance to reflect or think about the last year and they can make a poster of all the things you want to share that went well or did not.

"Got it." Ella and Lexi said.

"Great! Then the next day, we're going to talk about all the fun things we want to do and achieve next year. We'll each create our own special dream boards, present them, and then decide what goals we want to accomplish next year. Once we finish that, we'll go to a restaurant for lunch and do some other fun things. Then, on our last day here, we'll make sure we talked about everything that we wanted to and we'll complete one last fun activity. After that, we'll head home. Do you have any questions?"

The girls asked a few random questions like how long certain activities would take and what meals we would be making each day (like I said, we're foodies!). They also asked if we could do other fun things, like making s'mores and shopping. Rachel and I explained that as long we completed the main activity of the day, we should have time to do whatever else they wanted. Once there were no more questions, I mentioned that we needed to remember and practice a couple things while on this trip.

"If we want to have a lot of fun on this trip and plan the best next year ever, we'll all need to keep a few things in mind," I started. "For instance, we're all going to get opportunities to share our thoughts and feelings on this retreat. And when somebody is sharing, I would really like it if we could all be respectful when they are talking. This means we won't talk over each other, and we won't make fun of anything that anyone says. If we all commit to this, we can be a lot more honest and open with each other. And if we're honest with each other, we can understand each other really well and plan a year that will make all of us happy. How does that sound?" I asked.

"That sounds great!" was the unanimous reply.

I explained a few more "rules" for the retreat, but I made sure to present them like requests or suggestions. I really didn't want my family to feel like I was being too strict or serious, so I did my best to remain relaxed and loving as I went over these guidelines. I tried to emphasize that if we all behaved in these ways, we could eliminate the negative problems we've been having and could achieve almost anything we wanted. By describing the consequences of their behaviors (both positive and negative), I was able to motivate everyone to behave better on the retreat.

***

When you're ready to have this conversation with your family on the first night, there are a few things you can do to ensure it goes well. For example, you can communicate the activities and guidelines in a way that will best resonate with your family. To accomplish this, you'll need to identify and play to each family member's primary learning channel.

I learned about primary learning channels about five years ago. Once I began leveraging them, it was pretty remarkable how much it improved my interactions with others. I could tell that my conversations I had with my family, employees, and other professionals were much more impactful and effective. That's why I believe that if you understand and leverage the concept of primary learning channels, you can benefit from them too.

THE THREE MAIN LEARNING CHANNELS

Back in 1979, a few psychologists proposed three basic learning modalities that are still recognized today. These three modalities—

visual, auditory, and kinesthetic—are the main channels of human expression. We can use any three of these modalities to teach and learn, but every person has a dominant modality. In other words, we all have a preferred way of learning (whether we realize it or not).

As you review each of the modalities below, consider which learning channels best suit each of your family members.

Visual

If your dominant learning channel is visual, you learn best by seeing, observing and watching.

Characteristics of visual learners:

- Must understand the "big picture" before diving into an activity or project
- Prefer to watch demonstrations rather than following written instructions
- Prefer reading and writing, rather than listening
- Like art, colors, patterns, magazines, and books
- Make decisions based on looks (e.g. will choose to eat foods that are the most visually appealing)

How to accommodate visual learners:

- Bring visual activities like coloring, painting, and arts & crafts
- Create printable outlines, agendas, handouts, etc.
- Utilize storyboards, graphs, charts, and illustrations during the activities
- Minimize chatter and visual distractions during important conversations

- "Paint a picture" when describing activities, events, goals, etc.
- Use words like *see, watch, look, show, visualize, vibrant,* and *colorful*
- Provide journals for note-taking (as mentioned later on)

Auditory

If your dominant learning channel is auditory, you learn best by listening to others and talking out loud.

Characteristics of auditory learners:

- Love to talk and sing
- Love listening to music and prefer to have white noise
- Tend to talk to themselves, click pens, chew gum, etc.
- Get easily distracted by noise and sounds
- Forget faces but remember names
- Prefer to listen rather than taking notes
- Remember things better when they are repeated out loud
- Make decisions based on sounds (e.g. won't go into a store that's playing unpleasant music)

How to accommodate auditory learners:

- Bring auditory activities such as Family Feud, Name That Tune, and Catchphrase
- Review what they are going to learn in the beginning, and summarize what you've taught at the end
- Emphasize sounds when describing activities, events, goals, etc.

- Use words and phrases like *hear, listen, I'm all ears, tune in, that sounds great*
- Give them plenty of opportunities to ask questions
- Provide time for brainstorming sessions and discussions, but set time limits
- Repeat key points to cue when to take notes and to keep them alert
- Play music when possible, but minimize noise during discussions

Kinesthetic

If your dominant learning channel is kinesthetic, you learn best by touching, imitating and completing hands-on activities.

Characteristics of kinesthetic learners:

- Love to play games and sports
- Prioritize being comfortable (in clothing, when sitting down, etc.)
- Enjoy dancing, moving and being active in general
- Enjoy the physical act of taking notes
- Tend to focus on feelings, both emotionally and physically
- May unconsciously touch people when talking to them
- Don't enjoy reading or sitting for long periods of time
- Tend to doodle, fidget and slouch

How to accommodate kinesthetic learners:

- Bring activities such as Charades, Hacky Sack, and Play-Dough
- Provide highlighters, sticky notes, and colored pens or pencils

- Use colored markers to emphasize key points on flip charts or white boards
- Emphasize emotions and sensations when describing activities, events, goals, etc.
- Use words like *feel*, *touch*, *ambience*, and *atmosphere*
- Encourage hugs and cuddling
- Ensure the environment is comfortable (e.g. lighting, temperature, seating arrangements)
- Use rhythms, beats and songs when teaching or emphasizing main points
- Have them rewrite notes to remember or memorize things
- Provide frequent stretch breaks

If you're having trouble determining what a certain family member's dominant learning channel is, just talk to them about it! Don't be afraid to explain what you're trying to do and why, because there's really no harm in doing so. Then go over each learning channel with the family member, and ask them to decide which one fits them best.

If you would like more help determining your family's dominant learning channels, use Worksheet #8: What is Your Dominant Learning Channel?

Once you have a better understanding of how your family best learns, you can more effectively communicate the retreat plans and guidelines. For example, if your family members are more visual, you'll want to write down the plan for each day so that they can physically *see it*. If they are more auditory, you'll want to provide extra details and examples as you talk about each day *out loud*. If they tend to be more kinesthetic, you'll want to *move around* the room and emphasize how you *feel*. This way, they will stay engaged and pay attention.

Of course, there's also a chance that everyone in your family has a different dominant learning style. If this is the case for you, your best option is to do a little bit of everything. Don't think it's possible? Most public speakers, teachers, and salespeople do this every day! If they can master this skill, so can you. This may require saying the same thing three different ways, putting it in various formats, or providing different examples, but this extra effort will pay off. If you accommodate your family's dominant learning channels, the first dinner conversation will be much more effective. Everyone will be more engaged and open-minded while you're talking, and they will thoroughly process anything you say. As a result, they will be more prepared for the retreat and more willing to follow your retreat guidelines.

PRESENTING THE TIMELINE

After I finished going over the retreat at dinner, I told Ella and Lexi I had something special for them. I went into the other room and came back with four journals and pens. I gave them each their own special journal and pen, and I showed them the ones that Rachel and I had for ourselves. The girls instantly loved them and got really excited to use them, especially because both of their journals and pens were their favorite colors.

"Girls, as we complete different activities, you'll probably have a lot of thoughts and feelings. You can use these journals to write your thoughts and feelings down so that you can more easily remember them. And fortunately, we're going to start a new activity right now!"

I turned to Rachel and asked her to grab our family timeline poster. When she returned with it, she showed the girls.

"This is our family timeline!" Rachel announced with excitement. "This timeline highlights most of our major life events from this past year—including both the good and bad. Your dad and I created this for two main reasons. The first reason is so that we can remember everything that happened in this past year *before* we start planning for next year."

"The second reason is so that we can consider how these moments made us feel. If we understand which moments from our past we enjoyed and those we did not, we can better determine what will make us happiest in the future. Does that make sense?" Rachel asked. Everyone nodded.

"Great! So in order to understand how each moment made us feel, we're going to rank each moment based on how awesome or bad it was. But in reality, we probably have very different opinions on each of these moments. For instance, a moment that made me really happy may have actually made Lexi really sad. And something that really bothered Dad may not have bothered Ella at all. Instead of ranking them together, we're going to rank them individually."

Rachel took our family timeline and taped it up to a blank space on the wall that everyone could easily see. Then I grabbed four blank #2 Worksheets: Rating The Past that we brought and passed one out to each person.

"We'll use these worksheets to rank the moments on our family timeline. The middle section is where you will record your rankings. Now, do you see the markers on the left that say negative ten, negative five, zero, positive five, and positive ten? This is the scale you'll use to rank each moment. If you rank a moment as a negative ten, that means it was one of the worst memories of the year. If you rank it as a positive ten, that means it was like the best thing that happened to you this year," I explained.

"What if we ranked it as a zero?" Lexi asked.

"That would probably mean that the moment didn't really affect you either way," I answered. "You didn't love or hate it, and it didn't matter that it happened."

"Got it!" Lexi replied.

"Great! Let's talk through the first one together," I said.

"The first thing on here is New Year's Eve. When I think about this day, I first remember that Dave and Marissa invited me and Mom to celebrate New Year's Eve with them. I remember being really excited about it, but then Marissa got sick and our plans got cancelled. I was pretty bummed at first, but mom and I ended up having a really nice date night, so I got over it really quickly. Plus, we didn't host a New Year's Eve party like we did the year before, which was a major stress relief for me. So I would probably rate New Year's Eve as a plus four." After I finished explaining my answer, I drew the dot on my timeline.

"Rachel, how would you rate New Year's Eve?" I asked.

"Our date night was really nice, but I was actually pretty upset that our plans got cancelled. I also regretted not throwing another party because I really like big New Year's Eve celebrations. I would probably rate it more as a negative two," she admitted. She marked the dot on her timeline too.

"Lexi, how about you?" I asked.

"Well, Ella and I stayed at Grandma's on New Year's Eve, and that was really fun. We got to play with sparklers, had Grandma's amazing milkshakes and we stayed up really late. But I didn't get to hang out with my friends, and that was pretty lame, so... I would probably rate it as a plus five," she reasoned. Ella agreed with her, so they both put a dot at +5.

"Perfect! Let's take the next ten minutes or so to rate all the other events on our family timeline. Each new dot should be marked slightly to the right of the last one, as if you're plotting points on a graph," I explained. I knew Ella and Lexi have created graphs at school, so figured this was a good way of explaining it.

We spent the next ten minutes in silence, ranking each milestone on the timeline. After everyone was done, I helped Ella and Lexi connect all of their dots with a line. Then I laid all of our worksheets out on the table and glanced over them to compare our results. Our timelines had many similarities, but there were many notable differences as well. For instance, when I compared mine and Lexi's, the high and low points didn't correspond at all. We must have very different opinions on how this last year went!

"Now let's talk through each event and present our rankings," I announced. "We already talked about New Year's Eve, so let's go on to the next one. This one is about me getting the flu … Boooo!" I complained.

"I ranked this as a negative eight, because having the flu was by far one of the most miserable things that happened to me. All I wanted to do was hang out with you guys and go to work, but I could barely move or think straight. I definitely want to avoid getting sick again in the future."

"Why didn't you give it a negative ten then?" Ella asked.

"So even though I felt like a truck drove over me, and probably made Mom crazy with all my complaining, all of you were taking great care of me. I also took advantage of some of the down time as I started feeling better. I got really caught up on emails and reading."

After a brief pause, I said, "Rachel, what did you rate it as?" I knew Rachel ran a lot of errands for me when I was sick, such as getting me more medicine and chicken soup. I was really interested to hear if she enjoyed helping me, or if she was annoyed and thought I was being too much of a cry baby.

"I gave it a negative two," Rachel responded. "I didn't mind taking care of you, but you were pretty needy. I couldn't wait for you to feel better toward the end of it. I also kept thinking that if you took better care of yourself on a regular basis, you probably wouldn't have gotten so sick in the first place. Just keep that in mind!"

After I agreed with her, I asked Ella what she rated it as.

"I gave it a plus four, because I liked taking care of sick Daddy! I get to hang out with you *a lot* more because you can't work as much," she explained.

Ella's reply really shocked me, and it honestly made me feel pretty guilty. She likes it when I'm sick because she finally gets to spend more time with me ... If that's the case, I should really just give her more of my time when I'm healthy.

"But Ella, what if you could just hang out with healthy Daddy more often?" I asked.

"I mean that would obviously be the best! I like healthy Daddy a lot more."

"Then let's make sure that happens more in the future." She flashed me a big smile.

We had several more conversations like this as we reviewed our family timeline and compared our ratings. If our ratings closely aligned or drastically differed, we would spend some extra time finding out why that was. For instance, we would consider things like, "Why did all of us give that vacation a really low rating?" or "How come we all have different ratings for that birthday party?" And let me tell you, each of these conversations were priceless. They confirmed what works and doesn't work for our family, and how we can get along better. They also exposed more about who we are as individuals, and what each of our unique needs are.

Once we were done talking about the timeline, my head was spinning. I had so many thoughts, ideas and things I wanted to remember! I felt like I really needed some time to myself reflect on everything we just talked about.

"I don't know about you guys, but I have a lot going on in my head right now," I eventually said. "We just had a ton of great conversations and I feel like we learned a lot. Would you all want to spend some time writing down everything we just talked about?" I asked.

"I think that's a great idea," Rachel replied. The girls nodded in agreement. "Great! I would also love it if we could write down some past moments that we didn't discuss yet," I added. "They could be things we experienced as a family, or more personal memories we have from school or work. Let's just jot down some past moments that really stick out to us, and we can talk about them more tomorrow."

We spent the next twenty minutes journaling in private, which ended up making Ella and Lexi really tired. Once everyone was done journaling, Rachel and I got them ready for bed.

***

The timeline activity is the ideal first activity for your family retreat— and for more than one reason. First of all, it gives everyone in your family a chance to express their true thoughts and feelings about the past. By sharing your perspectives and opinions, you can all begin to better understand where you are as a family. You will also discover how everyone feels about your current situation and what they want to change most.

The timeline activity also encourages everyone to be more honest and vulnerable. In other words, it essentially acts as an ice-breaker. And when you're on a family trip that involves hard conversations, it's definitely best to break the ice first. This way, your family will communicate more openly and effectively throughout the retreat and long afterward.

It's also worth noting that this activity makes it *easier* to be honest. Think about it— directly asking your family members to share how they feel about the past probably wouldn't work. It's too general of a question, and nobody likes to be put on the spot. That's why it makes sense for everyone to privately rate specific moments before sharing their thoughts. It gives them time to self-reflect and think about what they want to say. In return, they feel a lot more comfortable opening up and expressing how they feel.

Finally, talking about moments from your past is the ideal first topic to discuss. If you skip this step and go straight to planning out your family's future together, it will be a mess. If you aren't aware of what's going right and wrong, you can't plan a future that will make everyone happy. You need to know your family's strengths and weaknesses, and you must be aware of everyone's unique perspectives and needs. This way, you can determine what kind of future will make everyone happiest.

In summary, when you're ready to present your family timeline on the retreat, start by saying what it is and why you created it. Then pass out the worksheets, walk them through the instructions, and give everyone at least twenty minutes to rate each event. Once everyone is done, go through every event and compare your ratings just as you did with your spouse. Ask everyone to briefly explain their ratings so that you can gain deeper insight, and consider what these new insights mean for your family.

If you feel like the worksheets won't resonate well with your family, or if you feel like they won't provide additional value, feel free to have an organic conversation about your timeline instead. You could even ask everyone to rate the moments aloud, rather than writing them all down. Just be sure to ask a lot of questions so that you can learn more about your family and start identifying ways to improve.

Here are some questions you can ask to gain more out of the timeline conversation:

- Can you walk me through your perspective of this event?
- What prevented you from giving this event a perfect score?
- What could have made this event better for you?
- If you could only change one thing about this event, what would you have changed?
- Is this an event you would want to happen again in the future? Why or why not?
- How did this event affect how you feel about [something/someone]?

Once you've reviewed every event on your timeline, spend the next thirty minutes or so writing in your journals. Encourage everyone to journal about how they're feeling and what they learned. Most importantly, ask them to make a list of other past events that really matter to them. This list will be especially valuable for the next day.

PRIVATE NIGHTTIME CONVERSATIONS

Once Rachel and I were officially alone on the first night, I realized this was a great time to have a private conversation with her and assess how she was feeling. We were both focusing so much on the kids all day, so I wasn't really sure what was going on in her head.

"So Rachel, how did you think today went?" I asked.

"I think it went surprisingly well for the most part," she responded. "The car ride was surprisingly easy, and dinner was really fun! I feel like the girls are being more responsive and cooperative than they usually are. It's pretty exciting."

I was actually thinking the same thing, so I started to contemplate why Ella and Lexi were behaving better than usual. Was it really just because Rachel and I had intentionally changed our attitudes and approaches? After we considered

****
"I FEEL LIKE THE GIRLS ARE BEING MORE RESPONSIVE AND COOPERATIVE THAN THEY USUALLY ARE."
****

this for a while, we knew that the answer was undoubtedly yes. We hadn't done anything else differently on this trip to encourage our daughters to behave better; our positive moods and reactions were the only new variable. Because we were communicating and acting differently, the girls were doing the same (whether consciously or not). It really opened my eyes to how much we really influence our children.

Rachel and I talked about what else went well that day, along with what didn't go so well. For instance, letting the girls choose their beds obviously didn't go over as well as we would have hoped. But fortunately, they were really cooperative when we calmly interjected and asked them to share the beds in the loft. Now we know that this "calm and rational" method can help us resolve fights! That means the real question now is: how do we avoid, or at least reduce, fights from happening in the first place? To figure out the most likely answer, Rachel and I started to reflect on what usually causes fights between Ella and Lexi in the first place.

Eventually we realized that most of their fights are always the result of disrespectful behaviors. Ella and Lexi tend to take each other's things without asking, they don't consider how the other sibling feels, and they often say hurtful things to each other. After we came to this conclusion, we decided to talk to the girls about the importance of respect in the morning. We also agreed to make it a theme for the whole trip, since most problems in general are caused by a lack of respect. Hopefully if we did this, our daughters would better understand the value of respect and would practice it more often.

Since we still had more time alone, I asked Rachel if she had any concerns about our plans for the next day. "Well, I'm definitely nervous about a few things," she admitted. "I just hope the girls are willing and able to do the activities."

I completely understood how she was feeling. "Well let's talk about which problems we are most likely to run into tomorrow, and then we can decide right now what we will do if they happen," I suggested. So that's exactly what we did.

One of the potential problems involved Ella. She's very young and sensitive, so we were worried that she would feel lost and overwhelmed when creating her reflection board. We were also afraid that she would be too shy to open up when presenting her reflection board.

We came up with a plan just in case this happened. If Ella started to struggle while creating her reflection board, Rachel and I would offer some specific, predetermined examples of events that she could reference on her board. And if she became too shy to stand

and talk in front of everyone, we would turn her presentation into a casual conversation that took place on the couch.

Our main concern for Lexi was that she might focus too much on materialistic memories rather than ones with emotional sustenance. Most girls her age tend to prioritize physical items over experiences, so we were nervous that her reflection board might be too surface-level. If that happened, Rachel and I decided that we would start a conversation about how money and possessions aren't everything. Hopefully, if we justified why physical possessions don't bring true happiness, she would be more likely to focus on the quality of life rather than the things she owns.

Rachel also brought up another point about Lexi of which I wasn't aware. Apparently, Lexi told Rachel that she was having problems with her friends at school. Two of Lexi's friends decided they didn't want to be friends with her anymore, which really hurt her feelings. Lexi had been really sad because of it and hadn't been sure what to do. Rachel explained that this issue would probably come up during the reflection board activity, so I should be aware of it.

I couldn't believe I didn't know about Lexi's friend situation and what she was going through. It reminded me that I don't know everything about my children, and they don't always tell me everything. I often forget that they might be struggling with things I don't know about. Fortunately, this retreat could change that. If everything went according to plan, my daughters would be more willing to open up to Rachel and me. As a result, we could understand what problems they are dealing with and figure out how we can best help them. Because Rachel and I really wanted to attain this outcome, we both agreed that we would be more honest and vulnerable with our children. By showing Ella and Lexi that it's okay to open up and express how you feel, we could motivate them to do the same.

These kind of conversations with Rachel went on for an hour or so, and I was incredibly thankful for them. Because we communicated our concerns to each other instead of keeping them inside, we were able to agree on how to handle various situations ahead of time. We were also much more aligned and prepared, and we felt a lot more excited for the next day.

It was also really nice to have an honest and private conversation with Rachel after being around the kids all day. I felt so much closer to her because of it, and I realized that this retreat could really strengthen our relationship with each other too.

***

If you want to strengthen your relationship with your spouse during this retreat, set aside at least one hour each night to have a private conversation with him or her. In addition to giving them the attention they deserve, these nightly conversations will enhance your connection and get you two on the same page before the next day.

Here are some other outcomes that will likely happen too:

1. Your partner or spouse will know that you care about their thoughts and feelings
2. You will identify and resolve roadblocks in your relationship and family
3. You will connect on a deeper level and get to know your spouse better
4. You will sleep better at night and wake up feeling ready for the day

5. Each day of the retreat will go more smoothly and be more enjoyable

If your kids are younger and go to bed pretty early, initiate the conversation after they've fallen asleep like I did. If your children are older and/or stay up later than you do, go on a walk with your spouse or just take them anywhere that's remotely private. Once you two are finally alone, start off by asking your partner how they're feeling.

If your spouse isn't in a good place, remember to be as understanding and supportive as possible. For instance, if they are upset about something that happened that day, take time to understand why. Don't assume that you know why they're feeling the way they are, and avoid changing the subject or talking about yourself. Just ask for more details and let them vent.

When they're done sharing, sincerely apologize if necessary and ask what you can do to help resolve the problem. Maybe they just need a hug, a massage or some time alone. Once they are feeling better (or if they already are), ask them how they think the retreat is going to get the conversation started.

Here are the three key questions you should ask and answer during this conversation:

1. What went well and what didn't go well today?
2. What should we do differently tomorrow?
3. What concerns do you have about tomorrow?

The main point of these questions is to reflect on the day with your spouse and learn from the events that took place. This way, you can identify the best ways to strengthen your family and relationship moving forward. You'll also reveal whether or not you need to modify your approach with your kids and/or other family members.

For example, if your family members were avoiding you or behaving badly all day, you'll probably want to come up with a new strategy for the next day. I'm not a family therapist, so I can't tell you exactly what the right strategy is, but I can suggest a few techniques that have worked for us and other parents we know.

Here are some parenting strategies to consider implementing if you haven't already:

1. **Don't react.** If you don't tolerate bad behavior whatsoever and you tend to overreact when your kids do something wrong, your kids might be acting out because they get more attention when they do.
2. **Point out the positives.** Celebrate and thank your children when they do behave well or listen to you. Doing so will reinforce the positive behaviors.
3. **Empathize.** Maybe there's a deeper reason why your children are misbehaving or not listening. Politely and directly ask them why they are not behaving to see if you can understand the true cause.
4. **Follow your own rules.** If you're telling your kids rules like they must clean up after themselves or avoid interrupting others, then make sure you're doing the same so that you are being fair.
5. **Explain your disciplines.** If you do need to give your kids a time-out or take away their things, make sure they understand why you are doing it and what they should have done differently. For example, you might say, "Son, I know

you were upset that your sister ate the last cookie, but hitting her wasn't okay. You should have just explained to her how you felt so she wouldn't do it again. Because you hit her instead, you need to go to your room for twenty minutes."

Of course, you are free to use all of these techniques during your family trip and at home. If you do, it's extremely likely that at least one of them will work and your kids will behave better. However, to avoid overwhelming yourself and confusing your children, just focus on testing out one or two of these at a time. Talk to your spouse about which ones are most likely to work for your children, and discuss how you will put them into action.

But remember, this conversation with your significant other shouldn't be entirely about analyzing the day and strategizing for the next. It should also be a time for you to both open up to each other about your relationship and family. Say what's on your mind and be fully honest with your spouse. If that means bringing up problems or concerns that you've been having for years, then so be it.

****

"THIS FAMILY TRIP IS LITERALLY THE IDEAL TIME AND PLACE TO OPEN UP TO YOUR SIGNIFICANT OTHER."

****

This family trip is literally the ideal time and place to open up to your significant other. You're finally alone with no distractions, and you're on a retreat that is all about *strengthening relationships*. If you want to talk to your spouse about something serious, this is your moment. Don't pass up this opportunity, because you will probably *never* say what's been on your mind if you do. Take advantage of this moment!

Whether you need to resolve marital issues or not, sharing your thoughts and feelings will help you two grow substantially closer. Being transparent will also strengthen your trust and respect for each other, which is something that every healthy couple needs.

DAY TWO:
REFLECTING ON LESSONS LEARNED

DAY TWO: STEP-BY-STEP

1. Eat breakfast as a family
2. Review the plans for the day again
3. Complete the respect activity
4. Create your reflection boards
5. Present your reflection boards
6. Enjoy the rest of the day as a family

STARTING DAY TWO OFF RIGHT

The next morning, Rachel and I woke up before the girls and made breakfast. We focused on being positive, loving and easygoing right off the bat, because we know that it's all too easy to be cranky and impatient in the mornings. And if you consciously start your day off in the right mood, it can improve your entire day. Don't forget that it's also contagious. Once Lexi and Ella woke up and joined us, I could tell that they noticed our positive attitudes and became happier as a result.

If you have a hard time starting your day off on the right foot, there are a few things you can do to enhance your mood early in the day. Personally, I suggest that you practice gratitude. If you recall and focus on a few things that you're grateful for each morning, you can get your mind in the right place. Even if you're not a morning person and you're never happy waking up, I'm almost positive this practice can help.

To get in the habit of practicing gratitude, purchase a "gratitude journal." You can buy a journal that guides you step-by-step through practicing gratitude, or you can buy a blank journal. If you do the latter, turn to the first blank page of your journal every morning and list three to five new things you are thankful for. Next to each list item, explain why you are thankful for it.

Finally, and probably most importantly, write your daily affirmation. What will make this specific day better? What do you want to think about and remember all day? This affirmation can be an action, fact, quote, etc. Just be sure to keep it positive and succinct. For example, it could be something as simple as: "Today, I am going to smile and laugh often."

Throughout your day, and anytime you see your journal, recall what you wrote down that morning and how much it means to you. This practice will help you maintain a positive mindset all day long, and can even cheer you up if something brings you down.

I got this gratitude journal idea from my friend Scott Novis who owns a national franchise mobile video gaming truck company called GameTruck and is also a member of the Entrepreneurs' Organization (EO). During one of our EO forum retreats, Scott gave everyone in the group a journal and a fancy writing pen. Next, he explained how we can benefit from journaling about the things we're grateful for each day. I honestly thought it sounded silly, but I tried to remain open-minded and told myself to at least give it a try.

That night, I started writing. I just jotted down a bunch of things that were going well in my life and expressed how I felt about them. I was shocked at how easy this was and how much it boosted my mood. Ever since then, I journal most days and my goal for next year is to do this daily. I am going to replace my daily To Do list with this process, which will allow me to reduce my "monkey brain" issues and remember what's really important.

Here's a page from my gratitude journal after just a couple weeks in:

What I'm grateful for:

1. **Hugs.** I absolutely love it when Rachel and the girls give me hugs before they leave for the day. Their hugs make me feel super loved and special.
2. **Diversity.** I'm so thankful for all the different types of people in my life. Diversity leads to so many unique and valuable ideas, opinions and skills.
3. **Wine.** After I had a really long day yesterday, I ended it with a really nice glass of wine. It was so relaxing, and it was the perfect way to end my day.
4. **Wedding invitations.** I recently received an invitation to Alix's (StringCan employee) wedding ceremony. I am so thankful that she actually wants me to be there for her big day.
5. **Opportunities.** I can't even believe how many new business opportunities I've been getting lately. I'm so thankful for every single one, and I'm even more grateful that these opportunities will truly benefit my business.

My daily affirmation: "I am confident in who I am, and I will prove this with my actions."

I usually start thinking about what I'm grateful for while I'm getting ready for the day. Then, while I'm eating breakfast, I write down five ideas that I came up with in the gratitude journal. I like to take my time and give it some real thought before writing anything down so that I can truly really cultivate a positive mindset. If I were to rush through it and jot down the first things that came to mind, it would defeat the whole purpose of the routine. By taking my time and putting some real thought into it, I'm able to truly boost my mood. Because this practice has benefited me so much, I have blocked off time on my calendar every morning so that I can make it a daily habit.

For that reason, give yourself some time to really think about what you're grateful for before you write them down. Whether you're getting ready for the day, commuting to work, or waiting in line for coffee, take that idle time to contemplate unique things that you appreciate. Once you have five good ideas, write them down. If you're not a fan of journals and you love technology, you can write out your five items in a notes app like Evernote, which is one of my personal favorites. Or, if you prefer, you could use a voice recorder app.

If you practice gratitude, here are some benefits you will likely experience:

1. **Encourages moral behavior.** You will be more likely to help and support your family throughout the day, and be more generous.
2. **Strengthen relationships.** When you become aware of the value of your family members, you are likely to treat them better.

3. **Minimizes envy.** When you realize that you are thankful for what you have, you are less likely to notice or be jealous of what others have.

4. **Minimizes negative feelings.** Most importantly, practicing gratitude dissolves negative emotions such as anger, bitterness or greed.

Considering the benefits that it offers, practicing gratitude can be an extremely valuable practice for your entire family. Feel free to share this technique and its benefits with them when appropriate.

TALKING ABOUT RESPECT

While we ate breakfast, I went over the plans for the day again to get us all aligned and focused. Plus, my children tend to forget things, so I knew that reminding them about our plans would be a good idea. After that, I decided it was finally time that I addressed one of the major problems we were having as a family.

"Girls, I want to talk about one really important thing first. Mom and I have noticed that we've been fighting a lot as a family, and neither of us likes it. How do you girls feel about the fighting we've been doing? Does it bother you?" I asked. They both quietly, and obviously, said yes.

"Why don't you like it?" I continued. Ella explained that she gets really sad when we fight, and Lexi agreed. Then I asked, "Why do you think we've been fighting so much?"

"Because you guys like Ella more than me," Lexi complained. I resisted rolling my eyes, but then Ella said, "Because Lexi is always so mean to me!" This isn't the first time I've heard these excuses.

I should have known that they would blame us or each other for the fights, but I really wanted them to stop thinking this way. No specific person is responsible for causing all our fights. Instead, as Rachel and I discovered the night before, it's really a specific behavior. We wanted Ella and Lexi to realize that the true cause of our fights is a lack of respect. But before I explained this to them, I wanted to understand my daughters' perspectives.

"Lexi, why do you think we like Ella more than you? And why do you think that leads to fights?" I asked.

"Do you remember that time when you let Ella have Paige sleep over, but you didn't let me invite anyone over?" Lexi asked.

"Yeah, I remember that. But we didn't let you invite a friend over because you were behaving badly that entire week. It wasn't because we like Ella more than you," Rachel explained.

"Well, still! Ella wouldn't let me play with them that night, and I got really mad. But instead of listening to me, you both yelled at me in front of Ella and her friend. That was seriously so embarrassing and unfair. That's why I yelled back at you and we started fighting," Lexi explained.

"Okay Lexi, I totally understand where you're coming from," I said. "But it sounds like the real reason we started fighting is because we yelled at you instead of listening to you. It wasn't because we like Ella more than you, especially because that isn't true. Would you agree?" I asked.

"Yeah, I was mostly mad you wouldn't listen to me ..." Lexi confirmed.

"I'm really sorry we didn't listen to you, Lexi. You're right, we should have heard you out instead of yelling at you," I admitted. She seemed really pleased to hear this.

I asked the girls for more examples of times that we've fought, and we identified the true cause of each one. Most of our fights usually began because somebody started yelling, saying mean things, being selfish, or blaming others. Once we agreed on what these common causes were, I was ready to explain how we could resolve them.

"Girls, I know exactly how we can resolve these types of issues—and it's super simple," I announced. "All we need to do is respect each other more. I'm assuming you know what respect means?"

They both replied with a meek "yes." After hearing that reaction, it was obvious that they needed a better understanding of it. I jumped up, grabbed some sticky notes and pens from the counter, and passed them out. It was time for an impromptu activity.

"Why don't we all write down some examples of what respect looks like, and we'll post them on the wall to help us understand and remember it?" I suggested. "Can you girls think of any?"

The room went silent. I could tell the girls were confused. Was I asking too much of them? I grew afraid that they were going to resist participating, and this whole weekend was going to be a huge mistake.

But finally, Ella broke the silence. "What about sharing?" she said.

Relief washed over me at that moment, and a proud smile stretched across my face. "Yes Ella! That's a great one!" I excitedly replied. I asked her to write it down on a sticky note, and then we stuck it onto the wall. We spent the next twenty minutes or so brainstorming more ideas and posting them up on the wall.

Eventually, we had about 20 ideas up on the wall. Some of the main ones included listening, helping, getting along, saying nice things, and caring. Rachel and I congratulated the girls for doing such a great job, and we asked them to keep these definitions in mind. We explained that if we all treat each other with respect, we will have a great weekend and a great next year. After this activity, I could tell that everyone was starting to get a little burnt out. I suggested that we take a ten minute break, and everyone agreed.

***

If you emphasize the value of respect on the beginning of day two, your family will be more likely to keep it in mind and be more respectful during the rest of the retreat.

The best way to get everyone interested is by explaining that respect can make your entire family better and happier. This way, your kids will associate respect with positive outcomes.

For example, if your kids often get into arguments because they take each other's things without asking (such as toys, clothes or video games), explain how respecting each other's personal items can prevent those kind of situations. If they politely ask to borrow each other's things before using them, fewer issues will arise and they could get along better.

Next, you'll want to ask, "Can any of you think of other specific examples of respect? Let's write them down and stick them up so we can remember them."

If anyone instantly starts complaining about the activity, explain that this is exactly the lack of respect you're talking about (depending on your family, you could say this in a jokingly manner or a serious tone). If they aren't willing to respect the activity and its purpose, everyone will be a lot more miserable during this trip. Politely ask them to change their attitude and be more open-minded so that your family can move forward. If they still give you a hard time, don't be afraid to be more stern and implement a new technique that you and your spouse discussed the night before.

Once everyone participates and you have at least ten sticky notes on your wall or poster board, be sure to thank everyone for helping out. Ask them to keep these examples in mind during the rest of the retreat so that it can be more enjoyable and successful.

WHO'S TALKING?

When my family finished talking about respect, we all took a ten-minute break. While everyone ran to the bathroom or grabbed snacks, I sat there analyzing the sticky notes on our respect board. I wanted to really ingrain the examples into my mind and consider how we could achieve these respectful habits. That's when I noticed that many of the examples we included revolved around communication: listening better, not interrupting each other, saying nicer things, etc. Clearly, we needed to be more respectful in our communication. I thought, "How can we ensure that we're respectful when we communicate?"

At that moment, I recalled two very simple and valuable communication techniques. Have you ever been in a large group of people and used some sort of item, like a football or baton, to give awareness to the person talking? Whoever is holding the talking item is allowed to talk, and everyone else is supposed to keep quiet and listen to the person talking. If you don't have the talking item and you want to talk, you calmly raise your hand to signal that you'd like the talking item when possible. Then, when the person talking gives you the talking item, you are free to voice your thoughts. It's such a simple concept, but it's extremely effective—and not just in very large groups.

Think back on past business meetings you've had with your team. Chances are pretty high that there were moments when everyone wanted to contribute to the conversation, so they all kept interrupting each other and talking over one another. Even if they always maturely decided who could talk first, a talking item can prevent these awkward situations altogether and streamline the conversation. Plus, imagine how many times more introverted team members have avoided speaking up because they didn't want to interrupt someone else or speak without permission. If you were using a talking item, these team members would feel less intimidated and more willing to contribute.

Finally, if you're anything like me, I'm sure you've experienced moments during meetings when you didn't realize how much you were rambling or confusing your team until a brave team member finally interrupted you and said, "I'm sorry, but I don't think any of us understand what you're talking about." If I would have used the talking item technique in those meetings, I can guarantee you that my team members would have felt much more comfortable raising their hands to shut me up even sooner. That could have saved us a lot of valuable time (and more importantly, stopped me from embarrassing myself!).

The same logic applies to your conversations with your family. Of course, you aren't *always* going to use a talking item at home (although wouldn't that be kind of wonderful?) but if you're ever having an important family conversation, or if everyone starts fighting and yelling over each other, the talking item can definitely come in handy. If you require everyone to be quiet unless they are holding the talking item, it will encourage everyone to listen better, avoid interrupting and stay calm. That way, everyone will be able to respect each other more and have a more effective conversation.

Your talking item can really be anything you'd like, but think about your family's personality, hobbies, and even inside jokes as you decide on the item. Try to choose something that will generate a positive reaction from everyone, because you don't want any of your family members to become agitated and hostile whenever they see it. It should also be something that can be easily tossed around and won't break on impact (so basically, nothing heavy or fragile). Finally, make sure it's something simple so that it won't be too distracting for anyone. I'd recommend using a stuffed animal, or maybe a small blow-up beach ball.

THE TOY BOX TECHNIQUE

As I mentioned earlier, I also thought of a second technique my family could use to communicate more effectively. This is a technique I use during my brainstorming meetings at StringCan, and it works every time. Whenever somebody brings up a great idea, or if they want to talk about something important that's off topic at the moment, we put it in the "parking lot." Your team may do something really similar, too.

The "parking lot" is essentially a poster board with sticky notes on it, and each of these sticky notes has one idea or conversation topic written on it. If we were having a meeting about our goals for the week, and a team member randomly asked if we could do a team charity event later in the year, that would be a little off-topic but still important, so we would write "team charity events" on a sticky note and put in the parking lot. Then, at the end of the meeting, we would readdress the parking lot items and have a conversations about the next steps. Sometimes we'll decide, "Let's talk about this at our next monthly meeting" or "let's do some more research on this in our downtime" or "let's figure this out right now." It really just depends on the situation.

There are multiple benefits to using the parking lot technique. First of all, it helps my team and I stay on topic during meetings so that we can complete our goals for each meeting. It also helps us remember important topics of discussion so we don't accidentally forget about them. It can also help us avoid having conversations at the wrong time or place, in the case that someone brings something up that I plan on addressing in a different meeting or perhaps a one-on-one. Overall, the parking lot streamlines our communication.

As I recalled the parking lot, I couldn't see any reason why it wouldn't benefit my family as well. When we have family conversations, we tend to interrupt each other a lot and change the subject without even realizing it. The parking lot could definitely help us prevent those tendencies during the retreat. But while calling it "the parking lot" is appropriate for work, I knew that this phrase wouldn't resonate well with my young daughters who don't even have cars yet. To make it more relevant and kid-friendly, I decided that I would refer to it as "the toy box" instead. After all, whenever my daughters need to put their toys or belongings in a temporary place, they usually throw them in the toy box. Considering that the parking lot also acts like a temporary placeholder, I thought this name change was pretty fitting.

If your family members tend to interrupt one another or get off-topic, I believe the toy box will really come in handy for you. Even if your family doesn't have these communication blunders, there's a good chance that new and unexpected topics will occasionally get brought up on the retreat. And if you want to address these topics at a different time, the toy box will come in handy. Just write the topics down on sticky notes and put them on your toy box poster board.

PRESENTING THE TOY BOX

When everyone came back from our five-minute break, I was eager to share my communication techniques with them. However, I didn't want to overwhelm them with too much new information, so I decided I would only bring up one technique for now.

After giving it some thought, I knew that the toy box would be the best tool to bring up first and before we start presenting I will suggest the talking item idea. We were about to recall a lot of past events and memories, and the toy box could help us stay focused on the past.

"Now that we're all back together, we're going to start talking about this past year. But before we do that, I want to mention something important," I stated. Once everyone's eyes were on me, I continued.

"All throughout today and this family retreat, we're going to bring up all kinds of memories, topics, and ideas. And sometimes we might want to talk about something that doesn't relate to the conversation or activity we're currently focusing on. For example, let's say that while we're talking about this past year, we suddenly realize that we want to do more adventurous activities together in the future. At that moment, we might be tempted to start brainstorming adventurous activities. However, that conversation would be pretty off topic because we are supposed to be reflecting on the past. And it's really important that we stay on topic so that we can complete each activity. Instead of getting off track, we would agree to brainstorm adventurous activities at a later and more appropriate time. Does that make sense?" I asked. Everyone nodded.

"But of course, it can be really easy to forget which conversations we want to save for later. So how can we remember and keep track of the conversations we postpone?" I asked.

"We could write them down somewhere," Rachel suggested.

"That's exactly what I was thinking," I replied. "And I think I know the perfect place to put them. Ella and Lexi, where do you put your toys when you want to play with them later?"

"Umm … in our toy box?" Lexi guessed.

"Right!" I replied. Then I grabbed a marker and a blank poster board that was sitting on the counter. In big letters at the top, I wrote 'Toy Box.'

"During this trip, this poster board will be our toy box," I declared. "But instead of holding our toys, it's going to hold our off topic ideas. Whenever we want to save a conversation for later, we'll write down the topic on a sticky note and put it in the toy box so we don't forget about it. Then, before we go back home, we'll make sure that we revisit and discuss all our toy box topics," I explained.

"Oh my gosh, I love that!" Ella commented. She tends to have a lot of random thoughts and ideas, so I figured she would appreciate the toy box. Rachel and Lexi also agreed that it was a smart idea. I was relieved that everyone understood the concept, and I was excited to see how valuable the toy box would really be.

"Great! Now that we all understand that, let's get into the main activity of the day," I said. "Does everyone have their journals?"

"Yep!" Lexi and Rachel replied together.

"Oh, I think I left mine in my room … I'll be right back!" Ella replied. She quickly ran off and returned with her journal.

"Alright then, let's get started!" I announced.

CREATING THE REFLECTION BOARDS

Once my family and I were ready to begin the first activity, I honestly felt a little nervous. I was really excited to get started, but I had *no idea* how this would play out. There was definitely a little voice in my head yelling, "This is too risky!" But I knew I just needed to tune it out. Even if this activity ended up being a massive fail, what's the worst thing that could happen? We would just be back to where we started. And while it would be kind of depressing that the activity didn't benefit us, I could at least tell myself that I tried. Once I realized that there was no reason to be worried, I was eager to get started.

"Here's what we're going to do today," I began. "Now that we've recalled some memories from the past year, we're going to create reflection boards. We're each going to take a poster board and some art supplies, find a place in the cabin where we'd like to work, and spend the next thirty minutes or so creating a personal collage that portrays our feelings about this past year. You can put anything you want on the board, but for some guidance, you can use events from the Rate The Past activity we did yesterday, as well as, focus on things that relate to family, fun, food and friends. Think about what you liked, didn't like, what you wish you did more of, and what you wish was different about these main topics. Do you think you can do that?" To my surprise, they nodded.

"When we meet back here at 11 o'clock, everyone will get a turn to present what they created and share anything they'd like to say. Do you have any questions?" The girls had no questions, and they seemed eager to get started. We gave them their poster boards along with magazines, scissors, stickers, markers, glue and other various art supplies that we brought. Then we all split up and got crafty for the next thirty minutes.

About fifteen minutes into the project, I walked around to make sure everyone was doing okay. Fortunately, both Rachel and the girls seemed to be really into what they were creating. They were all frivolously flipping through magazines, carefully cutting things out, and strategically planning how to lay out their collages. It was awesome and relieving, but it also made me realize that this might take longer than I initially thought... I should've remembered that everyone in my family is a perfectionist! I decided I would tack on another twenty minutes to the assignment, especially since everyone seemed to be enjoying themselves.

When I finished designing my reflection board, I walked around to see how everyone else was doing. I noticed Ella seemed frustrated so I asked her what was wrong. "I can't find a picture of clouds!" She exclaimed. She didn't even look up at me; she just kept hopelessly flipping through the magazines to find the right picture. I couldn't believe how determined she was to find a picture of a cloud!

"Why do you need a picture of a cloud, Ella? What is it representing?" I asked.

"I really loved the days when it was nice outside and I got to play in the backyard," she explained.

"Well, there's a lot of other things that can represent great weather!" I pointed out. "What about the sun, or a clear blue sky? You can also just draw a cloud on your board, or write the words 'perfect weather' somewhere. You don't necessarily need to use the magazines."

As soon as I finished saying this, she grabbed a blue marker and drew a big cloud in the corner of her board. After she was done, she looked up at me and smiled.

There's a good chance your kids or spouse might get stuck on something while creating their boards too, so check in on everyone periodically and see if they need help. Especially if they are taking a really long time to make progress on their boards, remind them that it doesn't need to be perfect and they shouldn't spend too long looking for one particular image. If they're having trouble finding an image they need, they may just need to think outside of the box or convey it with words instead. Especially if your children are very literal thinkers, you'll want to make sure they don't get too caught up in being super specific on their boards.

I also recommend that you give everyone a 30-minute, 15-minute and 5-minute warning so that they know when to start wrapping up. I found this technique to be very valuable for my family so that they were aware of how much time they were spending on things. Plus, I knew they would probably get upset if I unexpectedly told them to stop working!

Once our time was finally up, we all gathered in the family room. Rachel and I asked the girls how they were feeling and if they enjoyed the project. Lexi and Ella explained that they both had a lot of fun and they were very proud of their reflection boards.

"Well if you don't mind, I'd like to present first!" I said. I decided it would be best for me to go first for a few reasons. First of all, I thought I should set the stage for the presentations. I'm very comfortable with being honest, vulnerable and transparent around others, and I enjoy speaking in public. I figured that if I went first, the girls would feel more comfortable opening up during their presentations. I also wanted to intentionally bring up certain points so that we could discuss them as a family and find solutions.

"But before the presentations begin, let's go over a couple things first," I explained. This is when Rachel and I reminded the girls that we all should be respectful during everyone's presentations, which means that we remain quiet and listen while others are talking. After we briefly went over this, I introduced the other communication technique that I came up with earlier.

"Lexi and Ella, you know this stuffed minion toy that I brought with us?" I rhetorically asked, as I waved the funny-looking thing in the air. "This is going to be our talking item. Whoever is holding the minion is allowed to talk. Whoever isn't holding the minion is expected to listen to the family member who is talking. If you would like the minion because you have something you would like to say or ask, all you need to do is raise your hand. But please don't raise your hand every five minutes."

I realized I should remind the girls about their journals at this point too. "If you think of something you'd like to ask but the family member with the minion is in the middle of talking, you can write down your questions in your journal so that you can remember to ask them once you do have the minion. Can we all agree to do this?" Once everyone agreed, I got ready to present.

I stood up in front of everyone and held my poster board. As you'll see in the pictures, my board consisted of two main sections: Color Me Happy highlighted all the key positive moments, and Bums of the Year focused on the experiences I wasn't happy about. I reviewed the positive side first to recall my favorite moments. I spoke about some of my favorite trips and memories from the year, and mentioned how much I loved living in Arizona. Then I went onto the other side.

As I reviewed the not-so-enjoyable moments from the past year, I was very careful about what I said. I made sure to focus on myself, rather than blaming anyone else for the things that appeared on this side. For example, when I brought up the fighting problem again, I explained that it was breaking *my* heart that we couldn't all get along and that I felt badly I've been so impatient this past year. And when I mentioned lacking a healthy lifestyle, I said that *I* wanted to eat healthier and exercise more so I did not get sick like I did the other month.

Most of the things I shared weren't very surprising, but I made sure to divulge some unknown problems I've been having too. I hoped that doing so would encourage everyone else to open up too, which would allow us to understand each other better and connect on a deeper level. Also, if we knew what everyone needed help with, we could find ways to overcome both personal and familial struggles.

****

"I HAVE A REALLY HARD TIME RELAXING AND SHUTTING OFF MY BRAIN BECAUSE I CAN'T STOP WORRYING ABOUT ALL THESE PEOPLE AND THINGS."

****

One of the unexpected things I mentioned is that I've been having a lot of trouble sleeping this past year. "You know girls, I worry about you *a lot*. I worry about your happiness, success, and your future all the time because I love you so much and I want you to have amazing lives. On top of that, I worry about your mom, my friends, my business, my employees and so many other things. I have a really hard time relaxing and shutting off my brain because I can't stop worrying about all these people and things. It's like I have a crazy monkey brain."

My monkey brain comment got some laughs from the girls.

"I'm not kidding, that's really how I feel! And all of this worrying has been keeping me up at night, so lately I haven't been getting enough sleep. I hate being tired all day though, and not having enough energy to play with you when I get home. So, that's something else I wish I could change about this past year ..."

Ella and Lexi were both surprised and quiet once I finished talking. Rachel already knew this one, but this was the first time I had actually said it out loud. I could tell she understood the magnitude of my sleepless nights because I was more direct and open about it. She even raised her hand for the minion.

Once I threw it over to her, Rachel asked, "How can we help you sleep better at night? What can we do to help you relax and worry less?" I had to think for a minute, but I eventually said, "I think it would help if I knew that you were all happy and safe before going to bed myself. And maybe it would be smart for me to journal more, so I can clear my head." Obviously, I couldn't be positive that these solutions would work. But even just the fact that we were talking about the problem and possible solutions was a big step in the right direction.

***

When your family is ready for the reflection board presentations, gather together in the family room (or any room that is available and comfortable). Once everyone is ready to get started, I highly recommend that you are the one that presents first. Yes, *you!* The first presentation will serve as an example for everyone else, so it's important that it goes over well. Considering that you are the one reading this book and you just read all about my first presentation, you know better than anyone else in your family how these reflection board presentations should go over.

Plus, if you're an entrepreneur or business executive, you probably have a lot of experience giving presentations or taking the lead at meetings. And trust me, presenting to your family isn't nearly as stressful as presenting to professionals. If you can give important business presentations, you are well-suited for this.

When you're presenting your reflection board, the most important thing to remember is that you are acting as a role model for everyone else. Be sure to communicate and behave how you would like everyone else to during their presentations. But just in case you're nervous and you really don't want to screw this up, here are some other things to keep in mind:

1. **Start and end positively.** Start by reviewing your best memories, and then dive into your less favorable memories. After you've covered everything, explain that you are very thankful for this past year so that you can end on a positive note.

2. **Be transparent.** Be completely honest about your thoughts and feelings, and don't be afraid to be vulnerable.

3. **Pace yourself.** Don't rush through your presentation. Talk as long as you need, but avoid rambling. Keep an eye on the clock if necessary.

4. **Be respectful**. Avoid blaming others for past events or making hurtful remarks. If this happens unintentionally, sincerely apologize.

5. **Commit to communicating.** If you become hesitant to say or admit something, just push through it and say what you need to say. Remember that this is the best time and place to express your true feelings.

If you follow these guidelines during your presentation, you will encourage everyone else to open up during their presentations too. As a result, your family will start breaking down barriers and cultivating trust. This will empower your family to communicate on an entirely new level, which is a powerful and eye-opening experience. When this happens, you will likely learn new things about each other and discover how to enjoy life together.

In other words, if you present first and commit to being vulnerable, your family's potential will skyrocket.

***

After I finished presenting my reflection board, we asked Lexi to go next. Rachel and I figured that Ella would have a more difficult time presenting because she's really shy, so we figured she should watch at least one more family member present. Lexi happily skipped up to the front of the room with her reflection board, and was clearly ready to talk up a storm.

Lexi titled her reflection board "Lexi's 2015 Past Review" and broke it up into a good and bad section—very similar to how I designed mine (she's my daughter, after all!). On her good side, she had a treehouse and ropes course because she went on some really fun camping trips in 2015 and learned to step out of her comfort zone. She also had a birthday cake, a cruise ship, clothes, and the word "fun."

When Lexi started reviewing the bad side, it was challenging for me to stay quiet. I think Rachel and I were both eager to ask questions so that we could dig a little deeper, but obviously we needed to follow our own rule about remaining quiet while the minion-owner is talking. I wrote down my thoughts and questions in my journal, and saved them for the end.

Many of the negative moments that Lexi brought up related to social pressures. Just like Rachel had mentioned the night before, Lexi explained that her friends were being mean to her and didn't want to hang out anymore. She also brought up that the kids at school tease her a lot for her size, because she is undoubtedly the smallest kid in her grade. Rachel and I weren't aware that Lexi's size bothered her that much, and we had no idea that other kids were giving her a hard time about it. Knowing this really opened our eyes, and it helped explain why she acted out at school sometimes.

Once Lexi finished presenting, I raised my hand. She tossed me the minion, and I asked, "Lexi, did you know that I was the smallest kid in my grade when I was younger too?" After her eyes got all wide, she responded with a high-pitch "You were?!" I confirmed that yes, I was telling the truth, and I told her a couple stories from my childhood to prove that I could relate. "Even though it was hard sometimes, being the smallest definitely had its advantages. I could run, swim and climb much better than most of the other kids, and I was *really* great at playing hide and go seek." That managed to get a smile out of her. "Also, when I made it clear to everyone that my size didn't bother me, they decided it didn't matter too. So that was how I personally decided to deal with it," I explained.

"And then eventually I grew!" I decided to add. "Now I'm an average height and weight for my age, and I'm sure the same will happen for you. Just embrace being small while you can. But if you ever really need someone to talk to about this, just know that you can come to me and I'll be all ears."

Lexi seemed really happy to hear this, and she thanked me for sharing. It was such a great moment; I hadn't connected with her like that in a really, really long time. If I didn't know about the power of experience sharing, I probably wouldn't have considered telling Lexi that I was also the smallest kid in my grade. But thanks to Entrepreneurs' Organization (EO), I knew all about this technique and how to use it.

Usually at EO, we get into small groups and ask for guidance on certain situations that we're facing within our businesses. This invites other members in the group to share their personal thoughts and opinions. However, some of the EO leaders taught us that there are a couple problems with this practice. First of all, when we give advice to someone else, we are basing it off of our own personal experiences. As a result, the advice we give may not actually be accurate for someone else's situation. Also, when we *receive* advice, we typically assume it is good advice and we feel inclined to take it (otherwise, we're turning down great advice that someone willingly shared—and that can just seem rude!). But again, what worked for someone else may not work for us.

Instead of sharing personal *advice*, we should solely share personal *experiences* that relate to the situation. Once we share our similar experiences and explain how we handled them, the person who asked for help can use this information however they choose. This way, we provide further insight into the situation and offer potential solutions without being too pushy or opinionated. This technique also helps the person asking for advice realize that they aren't alone in facing this situation, which ultimately helps you two better connect and establish trust. At EO, we call this experience sharing technique the "Gestalt Language Protocol."

***

Before we moved on to Ella's presentation, Rachel and I asked Lexi a few more questions to better understand her thoughts and feelings on certain topics. However, we purposefully didn't pry too much. This was the first challenging activity of the weekend, so we didn't want to push the girls too much or mentally exhaust them right away. Rachel and I just asked questions that would encourage them to be a little more specific about their wants and needs.

We also didn't try to solve every problem that everyone brought up. Rachel and I were more concerned about getting important conversations started, rather than resolving all of our issues in one day. Plus, we aren't qualified therapists, so we didn't want to act like we were. Instead, we just focused on opening the gates to better communication.

Ella was up next. As she walked up to the front, Rachel and I made nervous eye contact with each other. I knew we were both desperately hoping that she wasn't too young or shy for this.

Ella was so sweet and asked Lexi if she would hold her board for her while she presented, and Lexi agreed. It was really nice to see them getting along. Ella's board consisted of four main quadrants: fun, not fun, good and bad. It was an interesting way of breaking it up, but we weren't going to complain.

Once Ella started presenting, it became obvious that she was completely capable of speaking in public. She stood up confidently, spoke loudly, clearly communicated her points, and even stayed on topic. She must have learned public speaking skills from school (especially considering all the times she presented book reports in front of her class). Or maybe she was just a natural! Either way, Rachel and I were both pleasantly surprised by Ella's presentation.

Some of the positive things she mentioned were our dog, the house, and our family. Later on, I said, "I know you mentioned that our family is great Ella, and I totally agree! But is there anything you can think of that would make our family even better?"

After she thought for a minute, she replied, "Well, it would be really cool if we could do more fun things together. Like, I really love it when we go to new restaurants and stuff!"

"I *love* going to new restaurants!" I replied. "I think we all do, don't we?"

"Yeah!" Rachel and Lexi replied.

"Great! Then how about we try to find new places to eat this year?"

"Oh my gosh, that would be awesome!" Ella excitedly responded. To ensure that I wouldn't forget about this, I wrote down "find new restaurants" in my journal.

When she was reviewing the negative quadrants, Ella brought up multiple things that related to school. She often gets frustrated with homework, especially when it comes to spelling and math, so Rachel and I weren't surprised. But we took this opportunity to thoroughly discuss and pinpoint what worked best for her in school this past year.

"Ella, can you remember anything that you did differently when you received good grades on your tests?" Rachel asked.

"I spent more time studying with you!" Ella explained.

"Well when we study together, I usually create flashcards for you and ask you to say your answers out loud," Rachel replied. "So maybe you should use flashcards and repeat the answers out loud more often when you're studying, since that seems to work for you. And of course, I would be happy to help you study more when I'm not working."

"I would like that!" Ella proclaimed. So we decided to end our questions there.

Finally, Rachel presented. I was very curious to see what she would share, so I leaned in with anticipation. Instead of creating sections like most of us did, she created a collage and either put a happy face or sad face next to each word or picture. Most of her positive items were similar to mine, such as date nights and family vacations. While some of her negative points were similar to mine as well, like health and fitness, there were a couple that surprised me—especially Thanksgiving.

Our 2015 Thanksgiving was different from prior years. Usually, Rachel and I prepare a massive feast for dozens of our family members and host Thanksgiving at our house. Rachel loves cooking and inviting family over, so hosting Thanksgiving is practically a dream come true for her. But for me, hosting Thanksgiving is just a major pain in the ass.

As I'm sure you know, accommodating dozens of family members is a lot of work. Whenever we would host Thanksgiving, I would stress out and complain too much. When Rachel's parents offered to take us to their Country Club for Thanksgiving in 2015, I was very happy. I didn't even consider that Rachel might be bummed about not hosting Thanksgiving because I was so thrilled about it.

But when she brought it up during her presentation, I finally realized that it actually bothered her a lot. I wanted to blurt out an apology and talk about it a bunch, but I restrained myself and wrote my thoughts down instead. Once I finally got the minion, I calmly and respectfully asked, "Why do you enjoy hosting events at our house so much? Is it the company, the cooking, the house ...?" I figured that if I could understand what she enjoyed most about it, I could gain a fresh perspective and we could possibly find a way to compromise.

"I just really love being with my family and friends, and I feel like we have the perfect house to make sure that everyone is entertained. So it just feels right and really fun to host." Rachel explained. "I don't need to have dozens of people over, but I would like to host a few events or holidays at our place throughout the year," she clarified. This information really helped. I decided to end the conversation there, and talk to Rachel about it more in private.

Once everyone was done sharing and asking questions, I could tell we were all a little tired. Fortunately, the reflection boards were the only assignment I had planned for that day. After we made lunch, we spent the next few hours doing fun activities like building snowmen, starting snowball fights, and playing board games inside. It felt great to just relax and enjoy being with each other after all of those conversations. I think we all felt much closer to one another, and the level of trust between us was growing stronger.

When dinnertime came around, Rachel made her delicious chili. While we ate at the dining room table, I asked the girls how they were feeling about the retreat so far. Lexi explained that she liked reflecting on the past year, and she had a lot of fun building snowmen. Ella mentioned that she loved learning new things about us when we presented, and she really liked that everyone was getting along. But she also said that she was really sad I wasn't sleeping well at night.

Rachel and I both took turns expressing our thoughts about the day too. We told Lexi and Ella that we were having a great time, and we were really impressed with their reflection boards. We thanked them for participating in that activity and for sharing as much they did. Rachel and I also explained that we would love it if we could continue communicating as we did during our presentations. If we could always be honest and open with each other, we could maintain the level of happiness and trust we were currently feeling.

Next, I reminded everyone about the plans for the next day. "Now that we've talk a lot about the past, tomorrow we're going to focus on the future! We'll create dream boards instead of reflection boards this time, and we'll talk about all of the things we want to accomplish next year. If we start thinking about this tonight and write about it, we can plan out some really exciting things for next year. Does that sound like a plan?" Everyone agreed.

Just like the night before, we each spent about 30 minutes journaling about our future aspirations. Since I'm a very goal-oriented person, this was initially really easy for me. I was able to list out dozens of goals! However, once I reviewed my list, I realized that most of my goals were business-related. I knew I couldn't only focus on my business goals, so I needed to brainstorm some more. Sadly, I *really* struggled to come up with goals that didn't somehow relate to work.

After about ten minutes of racking my brain, I realized what I was doing wrong. I was asking myself, "What will make me and my family better?" rather than, "What will make me and my family *happier*?" Once this occurred to me, I started thinking about all the small things that make me happy outside of work, as well as what everyone shared during their reflection board presentation. I also considered what I love doing most with my family, what my personal hobbies are, and what brings me the most fulfillment. Suddenly, it was really easy for me to choose goals that had nothing to do with work.

That night, we put on a movie and let everyone relax. I figured some downtime was much needed after such a long and eventful day. As soon as the movie ended, Ella and Lexi were clearly exhausted and ready for bed. Rachel and I tucked them in, and then we stayed up a little later to talk again.

The conversation we had this night was very different from the previous night. This time, we cracked open a bottle of wine and took giant sighs of relief. Neither of us could believe how well the day had gone. It honestly went a hundred times better than we were imagining. Remember how we both thought Ella was going to be too shy and overwhelmed? That wasn't even remotely true! We were also wrong about Lexi focusing too much on material items; she had very few physical objects on her reflection board.

Our assumptions for how the day would go were pretty off overall, and we couldn't have been happier about it. It just goes to show you that your fears as a parent can sometimes be unrealistic—and you don't always know your kids as well as you think you do. Also, children really are capable of behaving and communicating. It just requires some proper parenting.

After talking about what went well, we discussed some of the issues we ran into that day. I brought up the time that Ella got frustrated with her reflection board because she couldn't find a picture of a cloud. This reminded us to keep an eye on the girls during the Dream Board activity, in case they got stuck. We would hate for them to waste a good chunk of time looking for one specific picture.

Rachel also mentioned what happened when we were building snowmen outside. Ella and Lexi started arguing about how to build one. Each of them had a different strategy, and both of them made sense. But instead of agreeing that they both had good ideas, they just started bickering about whose was better. Rachel and I told them that instead of building one together, they should each build their own. That way, they could build their snowman however they wanted. This is what ended up happening, and it worked out just fine.

However, as we reflected on this situation, we realized that we probably should have made them work together. If we told them to build a snowman together, and to take turns deciding what each next step was, we could have encouraged them to cooperate and share. Because we separated them instead, they didn't resolve their tension or learn anything from the experience. They just focused on building the best snowman they could build on their own. We decided that moving forward, we wouldn't separate the girls if they start bickering. We would help them hash out their problems instead.

Rachel and I also discussed what our plan was for the following day with the dream boards. Our biggest concern was that Ella and Lexi would get too carried away with what they wanted to do next year. As you probably know, children tend to have pretty wild imaginations and can dream really big, which is usually a great thing! But when it comes to setting realistic goals and planning for the future, these traits can be a little debilitating. If Ella and Lexi's imaginations got too carried away, we knew that their dream boards would be filled with unattainable goals. Then we would need to break it to them that they can't achieve all of these things, and that would be really depressing.

To prevent this from happening, Rachel and I decided that we would have a very frank conversation with the girls before they started creating their dream boards. We would explain to them that their goals and plans needed to be realistic, which meant they needed to consider how much time and money their goals would require. I also wanted to explain *why* it's important to push themselves a little out of their comfort zones but still set realistic goals, which is essentially because it allows us to be more successful and happy— rather than disappointed. We both felt very confident that having this blunt conversation would work.

Another major thing Rachel and I talked about this night was our personal reflection board presentations. Now that the kids weren't around, we could have a more serious, adult conversation about some of the things we brought up. For instance, I was really eager to talk more about the Thanksgiving situation that Rachel mentioned.

"Listen, I had no idea it bothered you so much that we didn't host Thanksgiving this year. If I would have known it was that important to you and you enjoyed it that much, I would have said we should host it. So I'm really sorry I didn't consider your feelings and I let you down," I said with sincerity.

"We can totally host more events in the future," I continued, "But we both know that I have a really hard time enjoying being a host, especially with too large of a group. I'd like to compromise or at least find a way to make it more enjoyable for me. Could we do that?"

Rachel looked really pleased with what I said, and she could tell I meant every word of it. She thanked me for apologizing and agreed to compromising. After talking about different solutions, we decided that we would host only five events a year and keep the number of people that attend as small as possible. We also discussed what I would and wouldn't help with when we hosted events so that we could minimize my stress level. Overall, it was a great and very much-needed conversation.

Later on, we ended up asking each other a lot of questions about our relationship too. We talked about how romantic and intimate we are with one another, and whether or not it was enough. Both of us agreed that we needed more private time together. I also asked her if I was fulfilling all of her emotional needs, which most men would be terrified to ask their wives. But I knew this was the ideal setting to ask uncomfortable questions like these, and it's a question I often wonder about. Plus, I know a marriage can't work unless the spouses are fulfilling each other's needs. So why should we avoid talking about it? These kinds of conversations really do have the potential to save marriages.

Similar to the end of day one, you want to ask your family if they have any questions or concerns about how the day went over dinner. You also want to remind your family what the plans are for the next day. For my family, they enjoyed after some family fun time writing down in their journal some of their dreams for the next year before they went to bed. After the kids are asleep, spend some private quality time with your spouse reflecting on the day and any topics you want to focus on for the next day.

DAY THREE:
REIMAGINING YOUR
FAMILY'S FUTURE

DAY THREE STEP-BY-STEP

1. Review the plans for the day
2. Introduce dream board categories
3. Set parameters for dream boards
4. Create your dream boards
5. Present your dream boards
6. Establish goals for every family category
7. Find out where your goals align
8. Enjoy the rest of the day

ESTABLISHING THE FRAMEWORK

The beginning of day three was filled with positivity, excitement, and anticipation. We all knew we would be discussing our goals and dreams, and we were all really looking forward to it. Needless to say, this day was much less serious and nerve-racking than the previous day.

But to ensure that everyone understood why we were creating dream boards and how we were going to accomplish this assignment, I reviewed the plans for the day once again during breakfast. Repeating the schedule also allows everyone to have a realistic preview of how the day will go, which helps them mentally prepare for what's in store.

"Girls, like I mentioned at dinner last night, we're going to spend the next few hours creating our dream boards! Each of our dream boards will highlight our personal goals, plans and hopes for next year. We'll have about an hour to create our own board, and then we'll each get time to present what's on it—just like we did yesterday. After everyone presents, we'll consolidate our goals and refine them a little more so we know how to best achieve them. If everyone participates and contributes their thoughts, we'll be able to devise an effective plan for making this next year the best one yet! Are there any questions?" After everyone shook their heads no, I continued.

"To give you some framework and direction for your dream boards, I created a list of ten main categories that you can focus on. Almost everything we care about and do falls under at least one of these categories. The categories also reflect all of the things that are most important to maintaining a happy life and family." I reviewed each of these categories after I introduced them.

Here's an overview of our family categories:

1. Personal Development or Learning
2. Family
3. Public Service and Community
4. Money
5. Pleasure
6. Spirituality
7. Relationships
8. School/Career
9. Health
10. Social

As I went over each of the categories, I offered some examples so that the girls could understand them a little better. For instance, when I reviewed the School category, I brought up Ella's school troubles: "Ella, remember when you said you were having trouble with spelling and math yesterday? Establishing goals to overcome those troubles would certainly fall under this category and could be super valuable for you. Maybe you could make a goal to spend more time studying, or to test out different study techniques to see which works best."

I also offered multiple examples for the Health category because improving our family's health was a major priority for me and Rachel. I mentioned making healthy meals more often, eating out less, going on family walks, etc. And because both Lexi and I talked about our nail-biting habit the day before, I brought this up as well. "Lexi, remember yesterday when we agreed that biting our nails was something we didn't like about this past year? If we made a goal to stop biting our nails, that goal falls under this category too." I explained.

"But how does nail-biting relate to health?" Lexi asked.

"Well throughout the day, we touch things like chairs, tables, food, and the dog. All of these things are covered in germs, and these germs get on our hands. When we bite our nails, those germs get in our mouths and then into our bodies! Isn't that gross?"

A look of disgust appeared on both of the girls' faces, and they screeched out "eeewwwww!" After Rachel and I laughed, I said "Exactly! So that could be a great goal for the health category."

****

"AS YOU PRESENT AND REVIEW YOUR FAMILY CATEGORIES, BE SURE TO TIE IN CONVERSATIONS AND TOPICS FROM THE DAY BEFORE TOO."

****

As you present and review your family categories, be sure to tie in conversations and topics from the day before too. If you remind your family what they liked and didn't like about the past year, they will be more likely to choose goals and aspirations for next year that will truly make it a better year than the last. You should also clarify that these categories are just for reference, and your family isn't required to create goals for each and every category. Just ask them to keep them all in mind while creating their boards so that they stay on the right track. Also, if they follow these directions, everyone's goals will be much more aligned.

If anyone disagrees with the categories or feels like you're missing one, have a conversation about it and be open to modifying them. For example, if you didn't include a Meditation category, and one family member believes it's an important category to include, give them a chance to explain why and then see if anyone else in the family agrees. If the majority of your family members agree that the category is really important, then go ahead and add it. Another thing you could do is explain that meditation falls under another category you already have, such as Health or Spirituality. Either way, the categories aren't a huge game-changer, so be lenient.

SETTING PARAMETERS

As you know, Rachel and I decided that we were going to establish some boundaries for the dream boards. This way, Ella and Lexi wouldn't get too carried away with this assignment and would choose goals that are within reason.

When I was ready to initiate this conversation, I said something along these lines: "As we create our reflection boards, I definitely want us to be creative and ambitious. But I also want us to be realistic so we can actually achieve what we put on our boards. Otherwise, our dream boards will only make us sad because we can't complete anything on them! When you're thinking about the goals and experiences you want to accomplish next year, consider if we have the necessary resources to achieve them, such as the time and money."

This is the ideal time to discuss your family's financial situation, and I highly encourage you to do so. Especially if money is currently tight or your children have been taking money for granted, this conversation is pivotal on the retreat. But even if money isn't an issue in your family, being transparent with your children about your finances can deepen your level of trust. Also, teaching your kids about the right and wrong ways to spend money can help them be smarter with their money as they grow up.

If you've never talked to your children about money, you're probably very reluctant to have this conversation. But the fact that you've never talked about it is another pivotal reason why you need to have this conversation! This retreat is about strengthening your family, and that can't happen unless you have these hard conversations. You signed up for this retreat, so follow through with it. Otherwise, you'll only hold yourself back and let your family down. You don't need to divulge your yearly earnings or present your balance sheets, but you should certainly let your children know your financial status before they start reading their dream boards.

Here are some tips for talking about money with your kids:

1. Be honest but brief. You don't need to tell them more than they need to know.
2. Put money into perspective to explain its worth. For example, you might say that a vacation costs more than 100 dolls.
3. Don't be afraid to talk about your debt. Just be sure to explain what debt is and how common it is in our society.
4. Explain that money is earned by hard work; it doesn't just come out of a machine.
5. Mention that we often need to spend money on things we don't want to spend money on, like bills and supplies.
6. Clarify that money isn't infinite, so budgeting and compromising is key.
7. Ask your kids what questions they have about money.

During our monthly meetings at StringCan, I let everyone know where we're standing financially with a letter grade. For example, if we didn't lose money that month but we didn't reach our sales goals, I would tell the team that our grade for the month was a B. I now use this technique at home since letter grades resonate well with the girls. If we didn't buy anything crazy that month, contributed to our savings, and had extra spending money, I would let the girls know our financials were at an A at the end of the month. This way, anytime the girls want Rachel and I to buy something expensive that we don't really need, we can explain that we can't buy it because we need to get a A! Feel free to use this system with your family if you think it could work.

As you clarify your financial situation to your kids, explain how it affects the goals and experiences you plan for next year. For example, I knew that Ella and Lexi would aspire to go on all of these expensive, crazy trips unless I explained that it isn't in our budget. So, this is what I told them: "I know we went on a lot of fun trips and vacations this past year, but those trips cost Mommy and Daddy *a lot* of money. As a result, we can't afford to go on as many trips this year. We can definitely plan a few great ones, but we probably can't invest our savings into another international trip like Paris this next year. When we're thinking about trips we want to take, let's focus on the ones that are in the United States and try to limit it to a few destinations." The girls looked pretty bummed to hear this.

As I expected, Ella said "But Daddy, I *really* want to go to Paris! When can we afford to go?" Ella asked.

I hesitated for a moment, trying to think of the best way to answer this question. I knew I needed to talk to Rachel before I could provide a concrete answer. "I think that's something we'll need to figure out at a different time, Ella," I eventually replied. "Why don't we put that in the toy box and we'll talk about it later?"

Ella rolled her eyes, but then she ran off and grabbed the sticky notes. After she proudly placed a purple sticky note reading "PARIS!" with a cute Eiffel Tower drawing on it onto the toy box poster board, we got back on track.

***

Along with money parameters, you'll also want to set parameters around time and capacity. Sometimes children can't fully grasp or just don't consider how much time it takes to achieve certain goals, so they set irrational deadlines and take on more than they can handle. To avoid this outcome, clarify that it takes a lot of time and dedication to achieve goals. For example, I know that Lexi has always been interested in learning a new language. But I've always worried that she doesn't understand how long it will take her to do so, or how much effort it will require. When I talked about time parameters, I brought it up as an example.

"Another thing to remember is that this board is only for the next year, and we can't accomplish everything in one year. It takes a lot of time to accomplish goals, and we all have very limited free time already. Just focus on the goals and experiences that are most important to you right now, and choose ones that can be completed in this next year. Consider how much time each plan will require too, and think about if you will have the capacity to take it on." I explained. Then I turned to Lexi.

"Lexi, I know that you've been wanting to learn a new language, and that's an awesome goal! But I just want to remind you that learning a new language is a time-consuming process. You'll probably need to commit at least an hour a day to studying and practicing if you want to make good progress this next year, which would mean you have less time for other activities like singing and swimming. Just think about what's most important to you and what's most worth your time. I would love for you to learn a new language but that may be more of a two-year goal that you start next year."

When you have this conversation with your family, I highly recommend that you use examples too. Bring up goals and plans that you know your children and spouse are likely to put on their boards, and explain how much time (and money) they will require.

Once you've gone over your categories and set your parameters, you're ready to create your dream boards!

CREATING THE DREAM BOARDS

When everyone was finally ready to create their dream boards, we each took our reflection boards from the day before and flipped them over. Rachel and I decided that we didn't need separate poster boards for each day, so using the back of the reflection boards would work just fine. We brought out the supplies from the day before too, along with a couple new magazines. After we ensured that everyone had the supplies they needed, we all spread out throughout the cabin and spent the next hour creating our boards.

Every fifteen minutes or so, I walked around to see how everyone was doing. When I walked over to Lexi, I noticed that she was cutting out multiple pictures of friends smiling and laughing.

"Why are you cutting out all these pictures of children, Lexi?" I asked.

"I really, *really* want to make more friends this year," she stressed.

"Oh okay. Why exactly do you want to make more friends?" I replied.

"I just wish I had more people to sit with and talk to at lunch. And I want friends I can go to when I need help with homework or other things," Lexi explained.

"That makes sense. How would you feel if you had more friends?" I asked.

"Umm … I would definitely be happier. And I'd feel better at school and have more fun!" Lexi answered.

"Great! Those are probably the *real* reasons why you want friends, right? Maybe you could portray those feelings on your board too. You could include pictures of two people hugging, or kids in your class working together. That way, you don't have duplicate pictures on your vision board and you can include various things that will truly make you happy. Does that make sense?" I said.

"Yeah! I like those ideas!" Lexi excitedly replied.

After we had this conversation, I realized it had two major benefits. First of all, by asking Lexi *why* she wants to make new friends, I pushed her to consider whether or not this goal would really bring her true happiness. Fortunately, she was able to justify that making new friends would make her feel happy, accepted and supported. We both knew that this was a reasonable and important goal for her.

****
"I WAS ABLE TO CLARIFY THAT OUR DREAM BOARDS CAN INCLUDE MORE THAN JUST PHYSICAL THINGS WE WANT TO ATTAIN AND DO."
****

Thanks to this conversation with Lexi, I was also able to clarify that our dream boards can include more than just physical things we want to attain and do. They should also reflect how we want to *feel* in the next year, such as feeling healthier, happier, more confident or loved. After all, it really doesn't matter how many friends Lexi makes in the next year. What really matters is that she feels happy, accepted, and supported. Because I pointed this out to her, Lexi portrayed certain positive feelings on her dream board along with physical things that could generate these feelings.

Now, looking back on it, I wish I had communicated these two key points to everyone in my family before we started creating our dream boards. But fortunately, because you haven't started following this roadmap yet, you can! Learn from my mistakes, and teach everyone in your family what I taught Lexi before you begin creating your dream boards.

Most importantly, ask your family to consider why they are putting each item on their dream board before they do. Is it because this item will generate some level of happiness, success, or fulfillment? If not, then the goal probably doesn't have a valuable purpose. And what's the point of pursuing a goal that doesn't produce positive results? If your family thinks this way while creating their boards, they can avoid establishing goals that won't offer any value. They will also clearly understand why they want to achieve each of the goals on their boards, which will make the goals more meaningful and important to them.

Finally, emphasize to your family that these vision boards can also convey how you want to feel in the next year. What personality traits, emotions or mindsets do they want to adopt in this next year? For example, maybe they want to be more adventurous, positive, or disciplined. Or perhaps they want to feel more excited, energetic or determined. These characteristics can definitely be conveyed on their dream boards.

When you are checking on each family member every fifteen minutes or so, if it's clear that someone getting off track, remind them to contemplate why they want to achieve certain goals. Ask them specific questions, and provide examples to guide them in the right direction—just as I did with Lexi. This way, everyone in your family will successfully complete their dream boards.

Don't forget to give everyone 30-minute, 15-minute and 5-minute warnings too. If more than one person still needs more time when the clock is about to run out, give them some extra time. Unless you are on a tight schedule, remember that there's no harm in being patient and understanding.

PRESENTING THE DREAM BOARDS

Once everyone was done creating their dream boards, we all got together in the family room to get ready for the presentations. Everyone seemed really proud of their boards and excited to share them, but I knew we couldn't jump into the presentations quite yet. I still needed to clarify a few things.

"Before we start presenting, I need to explain a few things first. These presentations will be very similar to yesterday's, but they will have an important difference. We'll each get a turn to present, and we'll save our questions for the end like we usually do, but we'll need to do one more thing. After each presentation is over, we're going to review and refine each of the goals that the presenter mentioned. We want to make sure that the goals we ultimately commit to are specific and measurable," I stated.

"Why do we need to do that?" Ella asked.

"I'm glad you asked!" I replied. "Our goals need to be specific and measurable so that we can ensure we're making the right amount of progress on them. For instance, if I said I'm going to start working out more, that's too vague to measure. What exactly does 'more' mean? Does it mean one more hour of working out each month, or five more gym sessions every week? If I don't specify how often I will work out, then I probably won't work out as much as I should or want to. By making my workout goal more specific and measurable, I will know how much I need to work out to achieve my goal. I can also easily determine whether or not I'm meeting my goal," I explain.

"Are you going to work out five times a week, Daddy?" Lexi asked. I walked right into that one!

"Lexi, that question brings up another great point! As we refine these goals, we need to remember to keep them *realistic*. Choosing goals that are extremely difficult or impossible to achieve will only set us up for failure. And I truly believe that with all of the work and other goals I have, going to the gym five times a week will probably be a stretch. Plus, I'm only working out once a week as of now. How about if I commit to going a little bit more than that—say, two times a week?"

"Sounds great!" Rachel instantly responded. Her quick acceptance caught me off guard... Was I still being too ambitious?

"Okay, I will commit to that then ..." I said hesitantly. "But let's also remember that these goals aren't set in stone. If we find out later on that the goals we set are actually unrealistic, we can always adjust them," I added (just to be safe). Before presenting the dream boards, don't forget to mention this new part of the presentations to your family. Let them know that after each of their presentations, you're going to review their goals and make sure they are specific, measurable and realistic.

I'm sure you've heard of the term "SMART goals." These goals are Specific, Measurable, Achievable, Realistic, and Time-bound. Experts theorize that these kind of goals are more likely to be attained. You're probably wondering why I didn't mention all five of these factor to my family, and I have an answer for that. I was worried that if I explained all of these components to my daughters, they would have felt overwhelmed and confused. I just narrowed it down to the factors that I believed were most important, and I would suggest that you do the same. However, if you feel that your family would understand all five factors and would love to know about them, you are more than welcome to explain them all. What you decide to do is totally up to you.

Once everyone understood that we would be reviewing and refining the goals, I needed to bring up Worksheet #9: Keeping Track of Your Goals. "Okay, there's just one last thing I need to explain before we begin," I announced. "To help us remember all the goals we mention during our presentations, we're going to write them down on these worksheets. I have four of these worksheets so that we can each have our own. But it will be too hard to write down your own goals while you're presenting, so I'll write them down for you as you present. I will just need someone to write down my goals while I'm presenting. Who would be willing to do that for me?" I asked.

"I'll do it!" Rachel responded, so I handed her one of the worksheets. At that point, we were finally ready to begin the presentations. To keep things interesting and fair, Rachel and I decided to reverse the order from yesterday. Rachel would present first this time, then Ella and Lexi would go, and I would present last. I encourage you to change up the order for the same reasons too, but I still strongly believe that an adult should present first on both days. This way, your children or younger family members get an accurate and effective first example.

Without a doubt, Rachel's presentation was the ideal way to start off the presentations. She mentioned goals for almost every category, and they were all pretty specific and measurable already. Some of these goals included volunteering four times a year, reading one book a month, hosting two holiday dinners a year, and working out three times a week. As she shared each of these goals, she remained really excited and optimistic—even when she was talking about goals that would require hard work and undesirable tasks. She emphasized that although these goals would require things she didn't necessarily like, the end result would be worth the temporary dissatisfaction.

Out of all the goals Rachel mentioned, it was clear that one of them mattered more to her than the others: keeping the house clean. "I really love our home, so I like to keep it clean! Otherwise, it just doesn't feel good to be in and I'm embarrassed to have company over," she initially explained. "And lately, that's been the case more often than not. One of my goals is to make sure our house is more clean and inviting this next year. But this is a goal I can't do completely on my own. We all live in this house, so we all contribute to either how clean or messy it is. If I'm going to accomplish this goal, I'm going to need help and support from all of you. Would you all be willing to help me with this, so we can enjoy being at home more?" Rachel asked.

"I definitely am!" I replied. "I'm sorry, I know I've not been helpful here this past year. I'll make sure I'm picking up after myself from now on. Girls, do you think you can do that for Mom too?" Both Ella and Lexi responded yes, but I was hardly convinced. I was doubtful that they would suddenly start cleaning more at home just because we talked about it. Whenever we ask them to clean up and help with chores at home, they complain about it or make up excuses as to why they can't help.

"Do you really mean that?" I questioned. I'm sure they could tell that I was skeptical.

"Yeah..." Ella said quietly. "I mean I don't like cleaning, but I like it when the house is clean."

"Sure, whatever," Lexi added. "I just don't like it when you make me stop what I'm doing to clean. That really bothers me."

"Oh, well that's good to know," Rachel said. "Okay then, I'll make sure to give you plenty of warning from now on."

"Thanks!" Lexi happily replied.

When Rachel was done presenting, we reviewed all of the goals that I had written down on her worksheet. Since they were already pretty specific and measurable, we went through them pretty quickly. However, I realized we needed to clarify the cleaning one further. She had mentioned wanting the house to be more clean, and we all agreed to help out more often, but we never set a specific goal for it.

"How often do you think we should clean, Rachel?" I asked.

"Well, I'd love it if we could all clean for a couple hours every day!" she explained.

My eyes shot wide open, and so did Lexi's and Ella's. Did she really think we would clean every single day? I needed to mitigate this situation quickly!

"Honey, I really think that goal is too ambitious..." I said earnestly.

"Relax, I was only kidding!" Rachel admitted. "Although I definitely would love it if that could happen ..." All three of us took a sigh of relief.

"How about I create a chore chart and each week we can change who owns what chores? Can we all agree to that?" Rachel asked.

"Yeah, that's sounds good to me! Girls, what do you think?" I said.

"I guess that's fine..." they both mumbled. They definitely weren't eager to commit, but they knew it would mean a lot to Rachel. I wrote this goal down, but I knew that if it was going to work, we would need to find a way to make cleaning easier or more worthwhile for them. I decided that I would brainstorm some ideas and bring this up again later.

***

When Ella went next, I couldn't wait to hear what kind of goals and aspirations she came up with. I just hoped that she didn't get too carried away. Thankfully, she really didn't. She wanted to do things like volunteer at an animal shelter (because she loves dogs), get more A's on her spelling tests, read more often, and even eat fewer desserts. You probably think I'm making some of these goals up, but I'm really telling the truth!

I honestly think Ella's goals were more mature and appropriate than I was expecting because of the reflection board activity. Because she reflected on what she liked and didn't like about the past year first, her mind was in the right place when planning her goals for the next year. For instance, she decided she really wanted to do better in school this next year because she knows she really didn't like it when she received bad grades in the past. She also understood that this goal was realistic because we came up with some possible solutions the day before.

But of course, not everything Ella said was 100 percent realistic—especially when it came to how often she wanted to do things. For instance, she mentioned that she wanted to hang out with her friend Paige more often because they don't spend much time together outside of school. When we were reviewed this goal at the end, I asked, "How often do you want to spend time with Paige outside of school, Ella? And what would you like to do with her?"

"I think Paige and I should have sleepovers every week!" she responded.

You can imagine the look that shot across both Rachel's face and mine when Ella said this. Every week?!

"Ella, you and Paige are in the same school, so you already spend a lot of time together. So why don't we reconsider how much time you should spend with Paige? How often do you hang out with her now?"

"Um, like maybe once a month?" Ella answered.

"Okay well why don't we improve that time by just a little bit more? Like, how about you aim to have two play dates with Paige every month?" I asked nicely.

"Okay!" Ella harped. I was incredibly thankful that she didn't argue with that.

If anyone in your family ever pitches an outrageous goal, try to compromise and reason with them like I did with Ella. Letting them set goals that are a huge change or a major commitment will only increase their chances of failure. And you don't want your family members to fail; you want them to succeed and keep moving forward! Instead of taking massive leaps, make sure everyone is only taking small steps. You can help ensure that nobody is being too outrageous by asking the right questions.

Here is a list of questions you can ask to help everyone establish reasonable goals:

- How much time are you currently dedicating to this goal right now?
- How much time do you want to dedicate to this goal?
- How much time can you realistically dedicate to this goal?
- When will you have time to work on this goal?
- When this goal is accomplished, what is the benefit?
- What specific steps are required to reach that goal?

As we went through the rest of Ella's goals, I asked a lot of these same questions to make her goals more measurable. Surprisingly, they really helped us speed things up. By answering these questions and then defining the goal, we avoided talking about insignificant details or logistics. If one of us ever disagreed with a family member's goal, we calmly explained why we disagreed and then found a way to compromise—just like we did with my workout goal.

***

Next, it was Lexi's turn. Aside from goals like making the honor roll and spending more time singing, I noticed that most of Lexi's goals focused on improving relationships. The goals that mattered most to her included spending more time with her friends, making new friends, and playing with our dog Hudson more. She also emphasized wanting to have more family game nights with us, which I brought up again when it was finally time to refine her goals.

"So what do you like about family game nights?" I asked her.

"I don't know, I just like that we can be silly and play games at home in our pajamas! And I know we all love playing games." She was right; all of us really do love playing games—including myself.

"Okay, that makes sense! How often should we have family game nights?" I asked everyone.

"Can we pleeeeeeaase have a lot of them?" Lexi urged. "I really love them!"

"Rachel, what do you think? How often should we have them?" I asked her, since I wasn't sure how to answer.

"Well I wouldn't mind having them kind of regularly," she replied. "We all seem to really enjoy game nights."

I completely agreed. In fact, on a Friday night, I would much rather play games with my family at home than go to dinner or an event with my friends. I just really want to relax and stay home after working all week. Plus, game nights are a great way to spend quality time as a family, so I was willing to have them pretty often too.

"What if we planned to do them once a month, then? That's a lot more often than we have them now," I suggested. At that point, our family game nights were only happening once every few months, so I thought once a month was a reasonable upgrade.

Everyone was happy with that, so I updated the goal on Lexi's worksheet to read "monthly game nights." Shortly afterwards, I read another goal on Lexi's worksheet that lead to an important conversation. This goal was "Earn more money."

"There's a lot of things I want, and I know Mom and Dad can't buy them all for me. So I want to find ways to make money, so that I can buy all the things I want!" Lexi explained during her presentation. This goal of hers really impressed me, and it made me realize that our earlier conversation about money was already paying off. She clearly understood we can't just buy her everything, and she realizes that she needs money to attain the things she wants.

I was also really proud that Lexi wanted to *earn* her own money rather than just asking us for it. This means she understands that money

****
"MONEY DOESN'T GROW ON TREES!"
****

doesn't grow on trees—it's something that you need to work hard for. I could hardly believe that she was able to grasp that concept at such a young age. However, I was worried that *because* she was so young, finding ways to earn money might be difficult for her. After I read this goal of hers out loud, I went silent and started thinking,

"What could she do to earn more money?" I wanted to find a way to help.

"I have an idea," Rachel suddenly said. I didn't realize that she had been brainstorming too, so I was curious to hear what she was thinking.

"I mentioned earlier that I really need more help around the house. If you helped me with chores, I would be more than happy to reward you with an allowance. That way I can get the clean house I want, and you can get the money you want!" she explained. I thought this was such a clever idea!

"Really?!" Lexi squealed. "That would be awesome!"

"Yeah! And Ella, the same would apply to you. But we need to make sure your Dad is okay with this, because it's his money too." Rachel looked over at me.

"Oh, I'm all for it! I think it's a great win-win," I replied.

"Great! What are some chores you'd be willing to do, Lexi?" Rachel asked.

"Hmm. Well I don't mind taking care of the chickens, or helping you fold laundry," Lexi responded. Yes, we really do have four chickens.

"Great, then you can be responsible for those. And how about you, Ella?"

"I like walking Hudson!" she happily stated.

"Okay, well that's one thing you can do. How about something that's not so fun?"

"Um … Clearing the dishes off the table after dinner?" Ella proposed.

"Sure, I could definitely use help with that!" Rachel replied.

We talked about a couple more specific chores that Rachel really needed help with and distributed them as best as we could. When it came to the more complex chores, like cleaning the pool, I agreed to help out with those ones. By the end of it, the girls each had new weekly chores. Once we understood all the work they would be completing, we discussed as a family how much money they should earn.

"I think we should get twenty dollars a week," Lexi explained. "That's how much most of my friends get!"

Twenty bucks a week for chores?! Rachel and I made eye contact and inconspicuously shook our heads. I had a hard time believing that other parents would even pay that much.

"Lexi, that means we'd be giving you eighty dollars a month. I don't think we can afford to do that, and I don't think you even really need that much," I said.

"I agree," Rachel added. "That's *way* too much. In fact, I really think you only need to be making twenty dollars a *month*, which is five dollars a week."

Lexi clearly wasn't happy to hear this, as she put on her pouty face.

"How about this: we'll start with five dollars a week, and if it goes really well, you can eventually get a raise!" I suggested.

"Hmm … I guess that doesn't sound so bad," Lexi replied.

"Ooh, I want a raise!" Ella exclaimed.

"Well if you do a really great job and earn it, you'll get one!" I replied. I felt like such a businessman for saying this, but I truly believed that this was a great lesson to teach my kids. I just hoped that Rachel was onboard with this idea too.

"That is, as long as mom agrees with me ..." I added.

"Sounds good to me!" she confirmed. I was really happy to hear that!

The reason I'm telling you this story isn't to suggest that you give your children money, weekly allowances or "raises." However, if you want to teach your children how to start earning and spending money, I do think it's a pretty great idea. Especially if your kids are entering their teen years, teaching them how to earn and manage money can give them a huge life advantage. They will understand the true value of a dollar and be more responsible with their money as they grow older.

However, I know that for some parents, rewarding the children with money isn't practical. Especially if your income is barely enough to make ends meet, you may not be able to afford to give your kids an allowance. And of course, if your children are still very young, it doesn't make sense to let them handle money. I know that some people just don't believe in giving their children money too, and that's completely okay.

While rewarding your children with money is merely optional, rewarding your children with *something* is a must. Rewards act as positive reinforcement, so they encourage us to repeat positive actions or behaviors. If we don't reward our children for doing positive things, they won't be as likely to repeat these actions in the future. Heck, they might not even realize they're doing something right!

I'm sure there's been a time at work when your co-worker thanked you for doing some sort of task. Simply hearing "thanks" probably encouraged you to repeat the task in the future, right? I'm sure you've *also* experienced a time when you worked really long and hard on a project. Despite all your efforts, you received zero recognition for it. That probably felt awful, right? And you probably never wanted to do a project like that again! This is a great example as to why rewards and positive recognition are incredibly important. They make us feel good about what we've done, and they let us know what we're doing right so we can keep up the good work.

Also, just like us adults, children need to be incentivized to do things. If they know that something good will happen when they do something specific, they will be more willing to make that action happen. If you want to encourage your children to help you with a goal, find a reason why they should help. What's in it for them? How will they benefit from helping you accomplish this goal? It's just like when you're trying to sell a product or service—nobody will buy it from you unless they will gain something from it.

As an example, let's say one of your goals is to lose weight. You truly believe that in order to achieve this goal, you can't take your family out to eat as often as you do. This means everyone is your family needs to be okay with eating out less. In order to get them on your side, you need to explain how they will benefit from eating at home. You could say that it will help them eat healthier, consume less, adopt healthier habits, etc. By explaining how they will benefit physically, mentally or emotionally, they will be more willing to support you.

However, if your family loves eating out and your kids need more incentive than that, you may want to offer a more obvious reward. And while money can certainly be an effective reward, it's not your only option. Focus on choosing rewards that best fit your children's ages, personalities and hobbies. What is something that they would really love to have? Or what is something they always want more of?

Here are some other creative ways you can reward your children:

- More TV or internet time
- More studying or homework assistance
- Offer them candy or sweets
- Give them a later bedtime or curfew
- Tell them a bedtime story
- Give them more time for video games or other activities
- Let them decide what's for dinner one night
- Let them control what music plays at home or in the car
- Take them on a special trip
- Spend some one-on-one time together
- Let one of their friends sleep over
- Do their chores for a day

Just remember that rewards can be a touchy subject, so you may want to have a private conversation with your spouse about rewards before day three of the retreat takes place. Make sure you are both in agreement as to which rewards you are willing to give to your children, and which ones you are not. This is especially important when it comes to allowances and money. If you understand where your partner stands, you can avoid offering something to your kids that your partner might not be okay with.

As a final and very important note, always explain to your children why they are receiving a reward when you give them one. For instance, you might say, "I'm letting you drink soda today because you spent a lot less time playing video games this week." By explaining to your children why you are rewarding them, they will understand that what they are being rewarded for was a really good thing. As a result, they will be more likely to repeat the good behavior.

***

Finally, it was my turn to present my dream board. Some of the goals I portrayed on my board included going on date nights with Rachel twice a month, paying off our credit card debt by the end of the year, and scheduling another family annual retreat by October. Aside from these goals, almost everything else I mentioned either fell under the Health category or Personal Development and Learning category. This was an intentional decision on my part.

Over the years, I've heard from various friends, employees and family members that I don't take care of myself enough. And I know they're right. I haven't been to the doctor in over five years, I never reserve free time for myself, and I haven't accomplished a single personal goal of mine in years. I don't make these decisions intentionally; I think it's just who I am. I always put the needs of my family, friends and employees before my own. I just don't consider my needs as important.

While this can sometimes be a positive quality to have, it can also be pretty debilitating. If I don't prioritize my personal wellbeing or development, I know that my health, success and happiness will suffer. But it's not just about me. If I'm not living a healthy lifestyle or regularly improving myself, it ultimately impacts my family too. I can't be a positive role model for my kids, and I won't be nearly as enjoyable to be around. If I really want to strengthen and improve my family, I *must* improve myself too.

Because I was thinking about all of this while creating my dream board, I made sure to choose plenty of goals that related to my personal health and happiness. Some of these goals included exercising three times a week, reading one book a month, listening to two podcasts a week, and cutting out bread, candy and beer from my diet. Then of course there was the goal I was most excited for and passionate about: learning how to cook more recipes with my barbecue and smoker.

"I *really* enjoy barbecuing and smoking food for our family," I explained during my presentation. "In fact, it's one of my all-time favorite hobbies because I love everything about it! Searching for and trying out new recipes, preparing the food, eagerly waiting for it to cook, and of course—eating the delicious meal at the end. I also really like cooking outside and sharing home cooked meals with all of you. I was thinking maybe once a month, I can find a new recipe and barbeque or smoke something for dinner. Would everyone like that?" Considering that we're all foodies, everyone was thrilled about this idea.

As I explained my other personal goals, I began to get nervous that I was being too self-centered. Was I focusing too much on myself?

Did I have enough goals dedicated to my family and career? However, whenever I mentioned a new personal goal of mine, I could see everyone's eyes light up. They were clearly happy that a lot of my goals focused on me becoming healthier and happier.

After I finished presenting my dream board, I turned the floor over to Rachel. She wrote down all my goals on my worksheet like I had asked her to, so now it was time to review them.

****

"I'M REALLY HAPPY THAT YOU'RE FINALLY PRIORITIZING YOUR HEALTH AND HAPPINESS."

※※※※※※※※※※※※※※※※※※※※※※※

"First of all, your goals really surprised and impressed me. I'm really happy that you're finally prioritizing your health and happiness. I think we all are," Rachel explained. "But do you really think you'll be able to avoid candy, beer and bread entirely? I don't want to discourage you, but I know you. Those are like your three favorite things!"

"I mean, I'd really love to commit to that, but I guess you're right. I'd probably get really cranky if I cut myself off entirely. Maybe I could have one cheat day a month?" I suggested.

"Yeah, that could work!" Rachel replied. She wrote "one cheat day a month" next to the goal on the worksheet. Then she continued reading through my goals out loud so that we could ensure they were specific and measurable. Once we finished going through all the goals, I asked Rachel if she had any other thoughts or concerns about my goals.

"Well, I noticed you don't have journaling anywhere on here, and I know that you really love doing that. You said it helps you de-stress and reflect on everything. How come you didn't make it a goal of yours?" Rachel asked.

"Oh yeah, I guess I should have!" I replied. "I'd love to add that on, thanks for bringing it up. Maybe I could make a goal to journal every day?"

"I mean you don't need to do it that often, I know you've already got a lot of personal goals on here. How about three to five times a week?"

"Deal!" I responded. I was really happy Rachel suggested this goal because I knew it would benefit me immensely. I also liked that she was pushing me to spend more time on myself because it reassured me that I wasn't being too self-centered. By the end of it, I felt great and confident about the goals I chose.

I have a feeling that you can probably relate to me here. If you're an entrepreneur with a family, you're probably more concerned about your career, family and/or friends than you are about yourself. You dedicate all of your time to other people as a result, and you never reserve enough time for yourself. But just remember that if you do care about your career, family and friends, you *must take care of yourself*. Otherwise, you won't be as successful or influential. By ensuring that you are healthy and happy, you can excel in almost every area of your life and make a more positive impact. Remember that you are the common denominator in all of your life goals and priorities, so your health and happiness must come first.

If you really struggle with prioritizing yourself before your relationships, it could be because you don't have a strong relationship with yourself. Stop what you're doing every once in awhile and focus inward. Start building a better relationship with your own heart and soul. Prioritize this relationship over all of the others, and treat it like a friend that you never want to lose touch with. Check in with yourself often to make sure you're healthy and happy. And when the answer is no, do something about it. Cancel plans, go into work late, schedule that doctor or therapist appointment, or go somewhere where you can be completely alone. Don't ignore your personal thoughts, feelings or needs. Treat yourself like you would treat your best friend.

If you can relate to all of this, I highly encourage you to focus on your personal wants and needs while you are creating your dream board. Obviously your relationships are an important aspect of your life, but they aren't the only thing that matters. Take this opportunity to consider what area of your personal life is lacking most, and establish goals that can improve those areas. If you're concerned that you don't have enough time for personal goals, don't worry about that during the dream board activity. You'll find out later on in this book how to make the time.

ALIGNING YOUR FAMILY GOALS

You'll notice that on Worksheet #9: Keeping Track of Your Goals, there is a column titled "Category." This allows you to write down which family category each goal fits under. By filling out this column, you can see if there is a specific category missing goals that might need a goal created for it. This is a critical step to check because if you didn't have goals for a specific category, you might end up discounting and forgetting about that category throughout the year. Ideally for each category that is important to you and or your family, you should have at least one goal in that category so that we give that category proper attention.

After my family and I refined all of our goals, I went through everyone's worksheets to ensure each of us had goals in the important categories. As I went through mine, I discovered that I didn't have a goal for the Public/Community category. I let everyone know and then asked for some suggestions as to what I could do as we agreed during our family retreat that we wanted to give back more to the community next year. Lexi and Rachel mentioned a few community events for which I could volunteer, but I wasn't sure which ones most interested me in that moment. I simply made my goal: "Attend two community events in the next year."

When I finished looking through my worksheet, I went through Rachel's. I noticed she was missing a goal for the Spirituality category, so we talked about that for a few minutes and threw around some ideas. After giving it some thought, Rachel decided that she would have one Shabbat dinner a month. She had all the goals she needed once I added this goal to her worksheet, so then I went through Ella's and Lexi's worksheets. Surprisingly, they both had goals in every category. I guess they really knew what they were doing!

Next, I walked us through each of the categories and its related goals or activities. As I did this, we looked for similarities among our goals to identify how we could conquer the category as a family. For example, when I talked about the Pleasure category, I read all of the Pleasure goals on each of our worksheets out loud. This included things like traveling, camping, movies, singing, cooking, eating, shopping, etc. Then we had a conversation about which of these were most enjoyable to us and how we could accomplish them together.

We decided as a family that we care most about eating and traveling, so we discussed which new restaurants and places we wanted to experience. Everyone had an idea of a couple new restaurants they wanted to try, so we each named one and made it a goal to visit all four of them within the next year. The traveling discussion was really interesting because we all had our own ideas and opinions. After everyone got a chance to list a few places they wanted to go and why (and after Rachel and I ruled out the places that weren't realistic), we contemplated what our best options were. Eventually, we agreed that everyone would enjoy New York and Washington D.C., so we decided to visit these places within the next year. We all got really excited about this and couldn't wait to start planning it out.

Because we reviewed our goals for each of the categories like this, we were able to discover where our goals overlapped and aligned. As a result, we found dozens of ways to reach many of our individual goals together. Being able to make these kind of connections and commitments strengthened our bond as a family and empowered us to be more successful. It allowed all of us to get on the same page so that we could become a team. This simple activity made it feel like everything was really coming together.

When you review the goals for each of your family categories, find out how you and your family members can succeed in each category together too. What does everyone love to do in each category? What matters most to them? How can you achieve that as a family? What can everyone agree on when it comes to this category? Just have some organic conversations about the category and its goals to determine ways you can all work together. You may want to establish more goals as you talk about this, or alter ones that you already have. At the very least, just get a general idea of what everyone can do to support each other in every category.

Maybe you'll realize that everyone wants to limit their television time, learn how to cook, or wake up earlier in the mornings. When you find commonalities among your family members' goals, point them out and talk about how you will commit to them together. You can suggest ways to encourage each other, best times to work on the goal together, or strategies for making the goal easier to accomplish. This way, you can find some common ground and build a solid foundation for your family. As a result, everyone will feel more connected and determined.

If someone disagrees with something that everyone else in the family wants to do, ask them to explain why they disagree and what they would prefer to happen instead. If they aren't able to offer a reasonable explanation, they are probably just picking fights and being difficult for no actual reason. This can be extremely frustrating for parents, especially because there's no obvious way to resolve the issue.

If this situation arises on your retreat, the first thing you will want to do is clearly communicate how they are making you feel and what the result will be if they continue behaving the way they are. You might say something like this, "[Insert name], if you aren't able to justify why you are disagreeing with all of us, then you are being unreasonable and we won't be able to compromise for you. Unless you can give us a legitimate reason why you aren't happy with these plans, we're going to disregard your disapproval and move on."

If the family member does give you a reason why they are disagreeing, hear them out and consider the situation from their perspective. For example, let's say everyone in your family wants to commit to a weekly bowling night except for one certain family member. They don't want to participate because they hate bowling and they aren't good at it. Or maybe they just don't feel like bowling with the family is a smart use of their time. These are pretty valid reasons for the most part. In this scenario, I would advise against telling them that they need to suck it up and go bowling. Instead, try to compromise.

Follow these steps to effectively compromise with your family members:

1. **Understand their true needs and underlying motives.** In this scenario, maybe the *real* reason why the family member doesn't want to go bowling is because they lack confidence or they are trying to maximize their time. Determining why they feel the way they do will help you offer a more appropriate compromise.

2. **Define compromise.** Remind your family member what compromise is and why it is important. You may say that, "When we disagree, we must compromise so that everyone can be happy. In other words, we need to agree to make sacrifices or meet somewhere in the middle so that we can achieve a specific outcome."

3. **Give examples.** Explain a compromise that your family has made on the retreat or in the past to serve as an example

and to show how common compromise is. You might say, "Your sister didn't want to volunteer like we all wanted to, but she agreed that she would if we let her choose where we volunteer. That was a very smart and fair compromise."

4. **Offer choices.** Brainstorm and suggest at least two different compromises so that the family member feels in control of the compromise. For example, if the family member doesn't want to go bowling because they think it's a waste of time, you could let them choose between attending bi-monthly bowling nights or leaving weekly bowling nights early (e.g. after an hour).

5. **Ask for suggestions.** If the family member isn't willing to commit to any of the compromises you offer, ask them to suggest a compromise they are willing to commit to. If they can't think of anything, then explain that you can't and won't compromise.

6. **Make it official.** When/if the family member agrees on a compromise, repeat it out loud to ensure the compromise is clearly understood. Also write it down so that neither of you forgets or accidentally distorts the compromise.

7. **Say thank you.** Let your family member know that you really appreciate their willingness to compromise so that they are more willing to compromise again in the future.

THE FUN PART

Once you are finally done discussing your family goals, I'm sure you and everyone else in your family will be just as worn out as my family was. Talking about goals and plans for hours can be a little draining. Once you've completed this activity, take a breather! Thank everyone for participating, and then let them have some time to themselves. Especially if the activity got intense or if it you took you longer than originally planned, everyone is probably going to be tired of talking and being around one another. Give everyone some space, or do whatever will help everyone get back into relaxing vacation mode.

Once my family finished the dream board activity, we all went to our rooms to just wind down for about an hour. Rachel and I didn't even talk about how the morning went when we were finally alone in our room; we decided to save that conversation for later. Instead, we just let everything go for the time being and talked about what we wanted to do for fun the rest of the day. We decided to take the girls out to lunch somewhere in town so that we could get out of the cabin. Once everyone rested up and got ready, we piled into the car and drove off.

We got lunch at this cute cafe we found, and we all had a wonderful time. It felt like we were all so much closer and in sync with each other, which is probably why we were getting along better than we usually do. Nobody was fighting or complaining, and everyone was being a lot more positive and respectful. It truly felt like we were enjoying spending time together. I was so relieved and joyful that I could only hope it would last.

After lunch, we met with a local realtor to check out some available homes in the area. For whatever reason, Rachel, Lexi and Ella love to explore houses (especially ones that are brand new and beautifully furnished) so we knew that they would enjoy spending the afternoon doing this. As weird as it may be, they definitely did.

If you haven't ever gone house hunting for fun with your family before, you probably think my kids are bizarre. But just try it with yours kid someday and see what happens. We have always loved Pine and the area surrounding it so we were seriously considering buying a vacation home so this house hunting was also a good use of our time.

I know house hunting definitely isn't ideal for every family though. Especially if your kids are trouble makers or get really loud, I'd recommend spending the afternoon doing something different like taking them to a nearby park or playground. If they're "too cool" for house hunting or playgrounds, consider taking them to a local mall or coffee shop. You can always see if there are any fun attractions or events in the area too, such as a water park or concert (just make sure it's age appropriate!). Again, whatever you do as a family, just make sure that everyone is involved and can enjoy themselves.

We ended up eating dinner in the town too, and that's when the girls started asking more questions about all the goals we talked about.

"So when can we go to Washington D.C., Daddy? And what kind of fun things can we do while we're there?" Ella asked.

I glanced over at Rachel and we exchanged facial expressions that both clearly read: "What have we done?!" The girls were already overly excited and impatient for all the fun plans we mentioned earlier, but that wasn't our intention. Of course we wanted them to look forward to this next year, but we didn't want them to obsess over all the little details or build up expectations that were too high. I knew I needed to set things straight, but I really didn't want to crush their hopes or dreams.

I spoke up as soon as the girls got silent. "Ella, Lexi … I think there's something you need to realize about all these goals we planned today. They are all really exciting and I'm looking forward to every single one of them, but we can't give *all* of our plans our attention and energy *right now*. It will just distract us from focusing on the goals and plans that are actually relevant right now," I explained. The blank stares on my daughters' faces made it pretty clear that they didn't understand what the hell I was saying.

I figured I just needed to be more specific, so I continued: "For example, I know we're all really excited about the Washington D.C. trip we decided to take. But in reality, this trip probably won't happen for another eight or ten months. It's okay to start brainstorming what we should do and where we should go while we're there, but constantly daydreaming about our plans can be dangerous. You'll just get your hopes really high, and then the trip won't be able to meet your expectations. And that will make you really sad. Does that make sense?"

Their blank stares turned into sad, frowning faces … and I instantly felt terrible. How did I still manage to crush their hopes and dreams?! But then, Rachel chimed in: "Girls, Daddy is just trying to say that if you enjoy this moment right now, instead of moments that are really far away from right now, you will be a lot happier! Of course it's smart and fun to think about the future sometimes, but the present moment is always the best and *happiest* place to be. So let's just focus on enjoying this vacation!"

Rachel's pleasant and persuasive approach instantly instilled joy back into Lexi and Ella. They both started smiling and nodding, and Lexi replied, "Yeah, I really am loving this vacation!" Sometimes,

Rachel just really knows all the right things to say. If your kids can't stop talking about plans you discussed and promised earlier, try what Rachel did. Just remind them to focus on and enjoy the present moment, instead of investing all of their thoughts and energy into the future. This is a great opportunity to teach your children how to control their thoughts and how to acknowledge what is right in front of them. If your children have problems doing this, take advantage of this moment!

Especially in today's generation, not enough children understand or embrace the value of the present moment. Heck, not enough adults even do! My children fortunately understand it because Rachel and I communicate its purpose and value often. But we still need to regularly remind them to be more present. It's amazing how easy it is to ignore what is right in front of you. Our cell-phones, to-do lists and inner thoughts are major distractions. But if you eliminate distractions like these and fully take in what's around you, you will be more aware, present and at peace.

If you want to teach your kids how to be present, there are various kid-friendly activities you can do with them. Here's a few that I suggest you try out:

1. **Play "I Spy."** Ask your children to secretly choose a specific item in the room that you can see, and ask them what color it is. Then try to guess which item they chose. This will teach your children to be more aware of their surroundings.
2. **Restrict then Relax.** Tell your children to bundle up into a ball and squeeze every muscle in their bodies as tightly as they can for 30 seconds. Then instruct them to slowly

release all of the tension and lay down on the floor. This will help them get into a relaxed state.

3. **Touch and Describe.** Have your children close their eyes, and then hand them a random object. Ask them to describe what they feel (e.g. the texture, size, number of sides). This will teach them to focus on very distinct experiences.

4. **Play Charades.** Ask your children to write down five things they are currently thinking about or feeling. Then instruct them to act out the first item without using any words. Once you correctly guess the item, move onto the next item. This will teach your children to be more aware of their thoughts and feelings.

Whenever you want to use these activities with your kids, be sure to present them as fun games rather than mandatory assignments or punishments. I also suggest listing some of the benefits that these activities offer so that your children are more inclined to participate. For example, you could explain that these activities will make them more relaxed. They will also enhance the joy of the current moment and the quality of their lives.

***

After we talked to the girls about being present, the rest of dinner was noticeably more quiet and peaceful. Because of this, I decided not to recall our plans for the next day until we were driving home. When we were finally all in the car, I got everyone's attention.

"As you all know, the plan for tomorrow is to wrap up this retreat and drive home," I reminded them. "We'll have breakfast first, and then pack up our stuff, clean up the cabin, and head out around

11 a.m. But before we do, we'll have a couple last things we'll need to complete. I'll talk more about these activities tomorrow morning."

When we got home from dinner, we spent the rest of the night playing family games. We played Skip-Bo for most of the time, but we squeezed in a game of Life too. When Ella and Lexi were finally ready for bed, we realized that we had to figure out who would get the "best bed" that night. If you can remember, Lexi and Ella both wanted the same bed when we arrived. Lexi slept in it the first night, and then they switched the next night. But this was now the third night, and unless they shared the bed, one of them would get the bed all to themselves for an extra night. Knowing my girls, I really didn't think there was any way they would be okay with sharing a bed. I figured I only had two options. Either I somehow choose who gets the bed, or I flip another coin to make it a fair chance. But then I realized there might be one more option ... and that's when I called over Lexi.

"Lexi, I need to ask you something," I whispered. She looked up at me, clearly in a haze of tiredness. "So we need to decide who gets the best bed tonight. Do you think *you* should have the bed, or do you think *Ella* should have it? Because I mean, Ella's stuff is already in there. And I bet you could make her really happy if you let her keep it for the last night. But it's totally up to you," I explained. And I really wasn't trying to trick her into doing something, I was just trying to nudge her in the right direction!

"Yeah, she really *would* love it if I let her keep the bed ... And I kinda like the bed I slept in last night more anyway, so she can have it," Lexi stated.

"That's really awesome of you, Lexi! Why don't you tell Ella yourself?" I suggested. I knew Ella would be really happy to hear this, so I wanted to give Lexi the opportunity to tell her. I figured if she told Ella herself, she would remember how great it feels to give things to others.

After Lexi took a few seconds to think about it, she walked over to Ella. I couldn't hear exactly what Lexi said, but I could see Ella's face light up once she realized she had the big bed for another night. Then she wrapped her arms around Lexi and gave her a big hug. For me, this was definitely the best moment of all. Once Ella finally let go, I could tell Lexi felt great for what she had just done.

Eventually, Rachel and I tucked the girls into bed. Then we had our last conversation about what went well that day and what didn't, along with what concerns we had about the next day.

Considering you just finished reading all about our day, I'm sure you can predict many of the things that we talked about during this conversation. For instance, presenting our dream boards and refining our goals went really well for the most part. We all respectfully listened to each other, and then we calmly discussed which goals we wanted to commit to most. We didn't always agree, but everyone was considerate of how other people felt and we were all willing to compromise. Rachel and I were incredibly grateful for that.

Some of the things that didn't go as smoothly were when the girls were actually creating their boards. They both struggled a bit and needed extra time, so Rachel and I tried to pinpoint why this happened. I thought about the cloud picture dilemma that Ella had, and remembered that she was thinking far too specifically and concretely. If she would have thought more abstractly and been less picky about what she put on her board, she probably would have finished a lot sooner.

When I pointed this out to Rachel, we both realized that we should've told the girls to be flexible and creative before they started designing their boards. If we would have clarified that these boards shouldn't be perfectly accurate or picturesque, they probably wouldn't have been such perfectionists while creating them. We also should have listed all the ways they could convey their thoughts and goals on their dream boards (e.g. pictures, words, drawings) to get their creative juices flowing. Especially if your family members tend to be perfectionists, I highly recommend that you do these things before starting either of the board assignments.

DAY FOUR:
THE FINISHING TOUCHES

DAY FOUR: STEP-BY-STEP

1. Eat breakfast as a family
2. Talk about the toy box topics
3. Write future letters to everyone
4. Get feedback for the retreat
5. Schedule your first family meeting

After everyone woke up on the fourth and final day, we made breakfast like usual. But this time, it felt different than normal. While we were eating breakfast together, it was obvious how much happier and connected we all were. Now that we had discussed so many important topics and opened up to each other, there was a sense of synergy among us all.

At this point, I also felt very relieved to know that we had successfully survived the retreat. Rachel and I were just plain giddy that our plan had actually worked. We successfully completed all of the activities we wanted to, and each of them benefited our family in some way. We also had dozens of eye-opening conversations that revealed how we could effectively strengthen our family. When I started to reflect on these conversations during breakfast, I remembered that there were some we postponed having. Fortunately, the topics of these conversations were all in the toy box.

CLEANING OUT THE TOY BOX

Once we were almost done eating breakfast, I decided to bring up the toy box topics. "Hey guys, we still have some conversation topics in the toy box. Why don't we go over those together before we start cleaning and packing up?"

Everyone thought it was a great idea, especially Ella (most of the sticky notes were hers, after all). I grabbed the toy box poster board and put it on the table. Then I pulled off one of the first sticky note, which simply read "Paris."

In case you don't remember, Ella asked me when she could go to Paris right before we created our dream boards. I told her we would figure it out later, which is why this sticky note was in the toy box. As I stared at the bright purple sticky note, I realized I still hadn't talked to Rachel about Paris. I wasn't sure if we could or even wanted to take the kids to Paris in the future. I needed to buy more time.

"Ella, you wanted to know when we can take you to Paris," I began. "To be completely honest with you, I don't have an answer yet. And I really won't have an answer until next year, because I have no idea what our financial situation will look like a year from now. But if all goes according to plan and my business grows, there's a definite possibility that we can plan a big international trip in two years in 2018. So once we approach the end of 2017 at our 3rd annual family retreat, we'll talk about Paris again and evaluate whether or not it's doable for the next year. I just need you to be patient and focus on the other fun trips we have coming up. Can you do that for me?"

"Yeah!" Ella chirped. I took a deep sigh of relief, and grabbed another sticky note. This one read "Earrings." I had to resist rolling my eyes. "Lexi, did you put this one up here?" I asked, trying to remember its significance. "Yeah Daddy, you don't remember? I asked you to help me pay for new earrings when we got back home. Then you said we would talk about earrings some other time," Lexi explained. I didn't remember this conversation at all, but that definitely sounded like something I would say.

"Um, okay ... So you want to buy new earrings? How much are they?" I asked.

"I don't know, I think like forty dollars or something," Lexi answered.

"What?! Forty dollars for *earrings*?" I exclaimed. "That's a little excessive, Lexi. I don't think they're worth forty bucks. Is there something else you want that's worth forty dollars?" I asked.

"No! I *really* want these earrings!" Lexi declared.

"Well if that's how you really feel, Lexi, then you can save up your own money and buy them yourself," Rachel chimed in. "We said we would give you an allowance for completing chores, so you can earn your money that way."

"Ugh, I know that's what we talked about, but that'll take forever..." Lexi mumbled.

"Lexi, we aren't trying to be mean or unreasonable—we just can't afford to buy everything. But if these earrings are really that important to you, you are more than welcome to save up for them yourself," I explained.

"I mean you *could* just give me the money! But I get it. I know you have to budget or whatever," She explained. If we had never talked to the girls about money, or explained what budgeting is, I guarantee you Lexi wouldn't have responded like this. Once again, I was *really* thankful we had that conversation.

We continued going through the sticky notes until we addressed them all. Most of the topics were really trivial things that we able to resolve right then and there. Then there were the other topics that were more complicated or sensitive, which is partly why we postponed the conversations in the first place. But now that we had survived so many other serious conversations and had strengthened our relationships with one another, addressing these topics was no longer as intimidating. Instead of cowardly avoiding these hard topics like we initially did, Rachel and I were very honest and upfront with the girls. And of course, that means we sometimes said things that neither of them wanted to hear. But because we now better understood how to communicate with each of them, our daughters were much more receptive to our comments.

When you go through your toy box topics, this will probably be how it is for you too. Some topics will be easy to resolve while others will be more challenging. The more challenging topics will probably either require an awkward, unpleasant or serious conversation. In these situations, remember that you now have all the experience and knowledge you need to address these hard conversations! You can also refer to the communication tips offered in previous chapters if necessary.

WRITING LETTERS FOR THE FUTURE

When we finished going over the toy box items, I only had one last task in mind before we got ready to go home. To end the retreat on a very positive and inspirational note, I wanted us all to imagine how we would feel if we accomplished everything we talked about. If we

****
"I WANTED US ALL
TO IMAGINE HOW
WE WOULD FEEL IF
WE ACCOMPLISHED
EVERYTHING WE
TALKED ABOUT."
****

took some time to consider the amount of joy and satisfaction that our new goals and plans would bring us, then we would desire the outcomes even more and push ourselves even harder throughout the year.

I wanted to explain this idea to my family in a way that would make sense to them. While I still had everyone together, I said, "Girls, a year from now when we all accomplish these goals, what do you think that will be like?"

"We won't fight as much! And we'll have a lot more fun together!" Lexi excitedly shouted.

"And I'll be a better speller and get to see Paige more!" Ella exclaimed.

"We'll also be a lot healthier and the house will be a lot cleaner, which will make me one *really* happy mom!" Rachel added.

"Yes, all great examples!" I replied, "And these are all really important things to remember. So, I think we should write them down. But instead of journaling about them, I think it would be really fun if we all wrote letters to our future selves and each other. Then we can save the letters and open them on our next annual retreat next year."

"Why would we do that?" Ella and Lexi both asked, clearly confused as to the purpose of this assignment.

"Well, if we congratulated our future selves for accomplishing the goals that we set, I think we would be more motivated to accomplish them!"

"I still don't get it," Lexi admitted.

"Okay, let me give you an example," I said. "One of my goals is to lose weight. I might write something like this: 'Dear Jay, I am so proud of you! Over the last year, you worked out three times a week and lost fifteen pounds. I'm sure you look and feel so much healthier!' "

Then when I write a letter to your mom, I might say 'Dear Rachel, I can't believe how much you achieved this past year! You're still regularly attending book club, and you volunteered at numerous events. You're a rock star! Also, I have to admit that I'm so glad one of your goals was taking more cooking classes. My favorite dish you made was the crispy skin salmon. And I bet you're really happy that I stopped leaving dishes in the sink, because I found out that drove you nuts last year.'

Everyone let out a laugh. Then Lexi said, "I get it now! That sounds really fun!" So, I got up and went to find some loose leaf notebook paper, pens, and envelopes. When I returned and passed out all of the items, I gave a few simple instructions.

"Okay so we're each going to get four pieces of paper because each of us will need to write four letters: one to ourselves, and one to each family member. That's a lot of letters, so you only need to write a few paragraphs for each letter. And I'll give us about thirty minutes to do this. Does that sound fair?" I asked. Everyone concurred, and we all started eagerly writing away.

When you ask your family members to write letters to themselves and each other, you'll want to provide a few examples and instructions too. Feel free to keep your examples fun and light so that everyone understands the letters don't need to be super serious. Plus, this is the last assignment on the retreat, so you want to keep the assignment easy and positive. With that being said, make sure everyone also knows they don't need to write extensive, detailed letters. A couple paragraphs of positive statements and encouraging words will do.

When Ella finished writing all of her letters, she looked at me and said, "Daddy, am I allowed to decorate the letters now that I'm done writing? I really want to make them pretty!"

Lexi overheard Ella's comment and announced, "I want to decorate my letters too!"

I figured decorating the letters wouldn't do any harm, and it would make the girls happy, so I told them they could. But I only gave them about ten minutes to decorate them, considering we still needed to pack and clean. When the ten minutes were up, we folded up all of our letters and sealed them into envelopes. We also wrote "From: [name]" and "To: [name]" on the front of the envelopes to keep them organized. Once all the letters were complete, I asked Rachel if she would be in charge of them. I figured she would be the most trustworthy one considering she hardly ever loses things and she probably wouldn't be too tempted to peek at the letters. She happily obliged.

When you read them, as we did, to kick off your next family retreat you will want to set the stage with your family that you can each share what you learned from reading the letters. For my family, overall everyone loved it. Ella, our youngest daughter, was a little sad after reading her letters as she didn't accomplish all the items we talked about in her letters. We talked through her concerns for a few minutes and that made her feel a lot better.

After the letters were completed, we cleaned up the cabin and packed up our things. Soon enough, we were ready to hit the road. We loaded up the car and said goodbye to the cabin. It was certainly a bittersweet moment when I realized that the retreat was over, but I was definitely ready to go back home.

A BLISSFUL TRIP BACK HOME

The drive home was by far the most peaceful road trip our family has ever experienced. I could tell we all understood each other on a deeper level, which was empowering us to effortlessly co-exist. I think we were all pretty talked out by this point too, so the drive was quieter than I was anticipating. But I had absolutely no problem with that, and I don't think Rachel did either.

Right before we stopped for lunch, I started wondering what Rachel and the girls really thought about the retreat. Did they learn a lot from it? Did they feel as happy and peaceful as I did? Or did they feel like it was a lot of work? I knew I needed to get answers, just in case my impressions were totally off base. Once we stopped for lunch, I decided to initiate the conversation.

"So, what did everyone think about the retreat?" I asked. I figured it would be best to start with a pretty open-ended question.

Fortunately, all of the responses were positive.

"It was so fun!" Ella responded. "I really loved that cabin, it was super big and cozy."

"Yeah that cabin was awesome! And the snow outside was really pretty," Lexi added.

I knew I needed to dig a little deeper after hearing these responses. Otherwise, my daughters would have kept rambling on about how awesome all the trivial things were. I was more concerned with how they felt about the actual roadmap we followed!

"What was your favorite activity we did?" I asked next. That one ought to do the trick!

"Umm … I think I liked creating the reflection boards the most!" Lexi exclaimed.

"Why is that, Lexi?" Rachel asked.

"Because I liked thinking about all the fun things we've done. It made me really happy, and it made me want to do more fun things," Lexi explained.

"Yeah, and now we know exactly what fun things we're going to do!" I added. Lexi quickly agreed with me.

"I think my favorite part was writing the letters. I'm so excited to read them next year!" Ella said.

"Well what if we did this retreat again next year, and we read the letters at the beginning of the next retreat? Would everyone like that?" I asked.

"Yeah! Let's do it again!" Ella and Lexi both cheered.

Rachel was smiling, but she was being awfully quiet. I turned directly to her and asked, "What do you think, Rachel? Would you want to do this again next year?"

Instead of responding right away, she looked as if she was contemplating her answer. This got me worried. Would I need to persuade her all over again to go on another retreat?

But then she responded: "As long as we stick to completing our goals all throughout this next year, then I would love to!" Now my daughters weren't the only ones cheering. "Yay! Let's do it again!" we all acclaimed.

Once we calmed down, I thought about why Rachel said what she did. Was she worried we wouldn't actually accomplish our goals? Did she think that all the progress we made would be short-lived? That had to be it … and I honestly couldn't blame her. Our family had committed to a lot of things on this retreat, and accomplishing everything would be quite the task. But I didn't feel like it was an impossible endeavor; we just needed to make sure that we tracked our progress! And fortunately, I had already considered how we would do this long before the retreat began.

"But Ella and Lexi, I hope you realize what Mommy just said! We can only go on this retreat again if we stick to trying to complete our goals throughout this next year. That means we need to follow through with everything we've said on this retreat. Do you have any ideas as to how we can do that?" I asked.

There was only silence; neither of them could think of any strategies to share. Considering I already had a solution, I figured I shouldn't push them to answer.

"Well, I have a great idea!" I finally touted. "What if we got together once a month for a fun family meeting and reviewed the progress that we're making on our goals? And if we find a goal we aren't making progress on, we'll find out what we need to do to make that happen. That way, we'll definitely be able to do this again next year!"

"That sounds really smart, Daddy!" Lexi replied.

"Yeah! Let's do it!" Rachel and Ella said harmoniously.

"Great! I'm thinking we meet on the first Sunday of every month. As of right now, does anyone have any problems with that?" I asked— mainly looking to Rachel for validation as she keeps our family schedules. Everyone shook their heads to signal no. "Awesome! Then how about we have our first family meeting in a few weeks at the start of next month?"

"Works for me!" Rachel replied. Ella and Lexi nodded in agreement. I was extremely happy that we all agreed so easily, and I couldn't wait to see how our first meeting would turn out.

Once that conversation ended, I went back to my original plan of getting feedback on the retreat. I really wanted to get everyone's opinions and find ways to improve the trip, especially now that I knew we would be doing it again.

Here are some other questions I asked:

- What was your least favorite assignment on the retreat?
- What do you wish we spent more or less time on?
- What would you want to change about the retreat for next time?
- Where would you want to go in the future?

Everyone's responses were very insightful, but they were all over the place. And I'm sure it will be the same way with your family. When you're asking these questions, be sure to write down everyone's responses so that you won't forget what everyone said. Then, keep these responses somewhere safe so that you can reference them when you plan your next family retreat.

But honestly, getting feedback from your family isn't necessarily your top priority as you travel back home. Realistically speaking, your number one priority is getting everyone to agree to meet regularly. If you want to keep the retreat's positive impact alive, and if you want to ensure that everyone makes progress on their goals, it's essential that your family meets on a consistent basis. Otherwise, the retreat's effects will fade and nobody will feel accountable for accomplishing their goals. In other words, everything will go back to normal. That defeats the whole purpose of the retreat!

When a good time presents itself, get everyone's attention. Then propose the idea of meeting at least once a month to talk about the progress you're making. If you get resistance from anyone, remember what you learned about getting your kids to buy in. You just need to imagine you're trying to win over a potential client or make a sale. What can you say or do to make them more interested and willing?

After our first family retreat, I want to share with you that our family was very good about meeting monthly and making progress on our goals. Then school and work got really busy and the monthly meetings continued to get rescheduled or, worse, cancelled. We did not complete about 40% of our goals we set and I strongly believe it is because we set too many goals and we did not meet consistently and frequently enough to discuss our goal status.

This was a significant topic of conversation at our second annual family retreat. We agreed as a family that making every Sunday night a special weekly family night and discussing our goals and progress would result in a higher chance of goal completion success. After our second family retreat the weekly meetings are going very well and we are making a lot more progress toward our goals compared to the prior year. Due to that, I recommend you consider a weekly, not monthly, family meeting. Our weekly meetings are usually right before or after Sunday night dinners and only take about 20 minutes.

When it comes to encouraging family members to meet and complete their goals, here are three more essential tips for being persuasive:

- **Answer "What's in it for me?"** List more benefits that your family will gain if everyone meets on a regular basis, like support, better grades, more money, etc.

- **Highlight the consequences.** Offer more examples of what will happen if you don't meet regularly, such as disappointment or disrespect.
- **Offer a trade.** Tell your family members that if they agree to attend regular meetings, you will do something nice for them such as taking them out to dinner.

In regards to *when* you will meet, this is entirely up to you and your family. I chose Sunday night because that's usually when everyone is home and not distracted by work or school homework. I also know that Rachel, Ella and Lexi tend to have more free time on Sunday nights. Propose a date that will work best with everyone's schedules. If you aren't sure, ask everyone when they are usually free and try to find a time that works.

In the rare chance that you aren't able to find a time when everyone is free, make an effort to be flexible or get creative. Here are some questions to consider:

- Can you or anyone else possibly adjust their work or school schedules so that everyone can meet?
- Can you discuss your goals during dinner?
- Are lunch breaks an option?
- Could you use Skype or Google Hangouts to meet virtually if someone is away on a business trip?
- Can you start a group text that everyone participates in at a certain time?
- At the very least, can everyone agree to update their goal progress on a Google sheet or goals board that everyone can access?

Once everyone agrees on when and how often you will meet, decide when your first meeting will be! I suggest scheduling it out at least a couple weeks into the future so that when you get home, everyone has time to get back into the swing of things. Plus, as you'll find out in the next chapter, there is one thing you'll need to do before your first "family goals" meeting.

POST-RETREAT:
THE LONG-TERM PLAN

POST RETREAT: STEP-BY-STEP

1. Create family goals spreadsheet
2. Have your first family meeting
3. Regularly meet with family to discuss progress on goals
4. Modify goals or offer support when necessary
5. Hold each other accountable
6. Discuss common excuses and consequences
7. Regularly self-reflect

After we got home from the retreat and unloaded the car, it took me a while to process everything that had just happened. The entire retreat felt like such a distant and perfect dream, but obviously I knew it was reality. And now that we were back home, I wanted to ensure that what happened on the retreat really stayed with us. I wanted everything we learned and said to feel real and in effect.

That night, I resisted the urge to work. Even though I wasn't on the retreat anymore and nobody necessarily needed my attention, I knew that going back into work mode would send the wrong message. In fact, it would probably be the biggest mistake I could make after such an eye-opening trip. If I wanted the retreat to have a lasting impact on my family, I needed to remain a changed man. Otherwise, the positive influence that the retreat had on my family would quickly fade.

Plus, all I really wanted to do was be with my family anyway. I wanted to enjoy the newfound synergy we had in the comfort of our home, especially so that it would stay alive. And the constant pressure and desire that I usually feel to work wasn't nearly as overwhelming, so I could more easily resist it. I could almost mute that annoying voice in my head that persistently tells me, "Keep working, or you will miss opportunities!"

I was sitting in my room with Rachel that night, trying to debate what to do with myself. What else could I do to ensure that we wouldn't forget what happened on the retreat? I grabbed my journal and started writing vigorously, trying to brainstorm ideas for what should happen next. We would be having our family meeting in a few weeks, but what happens between now and then? This is when I realized that I needed to do a couple things before that meeting happened.

CREATING YOUR FAMILY GOALS SPREADSHEET

As I mentioned before, the roadmap my family followed on the retreat was initially inspired by StringCan Interactive's annual goals planning process. After my team and I go through this process and decide which goals to pursue, we create a final spreadsheet that lists all of our goals. This spreadsheet also shows who is responsible for which goals and what the expected frequency or timeline for each goal is. When we have our monthly team meeting to discuss our progress on these goals, we refer to the spreadsheet to ensure we address them all.

Because I know how valuable the goals spreadsheet is for StringCan, I decided to create one for my family as well. This way, we could stay organized and know exactly what to talk about at each family meeting. I already knew what each of our goals were because I had the goal worksheets from the retreat, so it only took me about ten minutes to create the spreadsheet. Considering that you will have all of this information too, it should only take you about ten minutes as well.

You can format your spreadsheet however you'd like, or you can copy the format that I used. If you prefer the latter, use Worksheet #10: Family Goals and Progress.

Also, keep in mind that this spreadsheet is just serving as a rough draft for your first family meeting. It doesn't need to be perfect, and you can modify or refine the goals later on if necessary. In fact, there's a very good chance that you will need to flush them out more during your first family meeting.

REFINING YOUR FAMILY VISION

As you know, Rachel and I established our family vision prior to the retreat—and I'm extremely glad that we did. This vision served as a guide throughout the entire trip, especially when we were talking about our future goals. Because I knew what Rachel and I wanted to get out of the retreat and where we wanted our family to ultimately end up, I was able to ensure that the goals we chose were right for us.

However, the retreat revealed a *lot* of new information about our family's personalities and needs. Because I had so much more insight and a better understanding of my family, I felt the vision statement needed to be updated.

Before the retreat, I thought that all my family needed to do was listen and communicate more effectively. But now that we had completed Part One of the roadmap, I had a slightly different vision in mind. We definitely still needed to work on our communication skills, but I don't think that was our core problem anymore. As I discovered on the retreat, we were having trouble communicating effectively because we weren't respecting each other. That's why we would interrupt each other, not listen to each other, and sometimes even yell at one another. In the end, really all boiled down to respect.

Because I now understood this, I slightly altered my family vision in my head. Then I turned this new vision of mine into a concise statement. Here is how it currently reads: "We will empower each other to be happy, healthy and successful by regularly behaving in respectful and loving ways." I decided that I would present this vision during our first family meeting to ensure we all agreed on it and remembered it.

Depending on how the retreat goes with your family, you may want to revise what you wrote down for your family vision too. If you gained unexpected insight on the retreat and had some eye-opening experiences, there's a good chance that the family vision you established before the retreat isn't as practical anymore. If you want to update your family vision, start by reflecting on your major takeaways from the retreat. What did you learn about each of your family members? How are you all alike? What are your common goals and priorities? What topics, values, behaviors, actions and/ or solutions came up often during the retreat? It may help to look through your journal to find common trends and answer these questions.

Once you know the answers, identify the major discrepancies between these answers and the keywords you wrote down on the Worksheet #4: Describing Your Family Vision. Then alter your vision as you see fit so that it better aligns with your answers. In other words, ensure that your family vision incorporates the keywords or themes that your family focused on during the retreat. Feel free to get your spouse involved in this process too.

Remember that your family vision should make everyone in your family happy and fulfilled if it's achieved. It should also reflect your family's unique personalities, values and priorities. If your family vision accomplishes these two things, it will benefit you immensely.

THE FIRST FAMILY MEETING

Eventually, the date of our first family meeting began to approach. A couple days before the meeting was supposed to happen, I reminded everyone it was coming up so that they wouldn't forget. I also read through the goals spreadsheet just to refamiliarize myself with them.

When the day of the meeting finally arrived, I won't lie—I was a little nervous. I was definitely excited too, but I was worried the meeting would be stressful, boring or unenjoyable. Unless we were all excited about the meeting and in great moods, I was sure that we would quickly lose interest in discussing our goals. So, in the hopes of getting everyone amped up, I completed one of my goals and tried out a new BBQ rib recipe before the meeting. Fortunately, this turned out to be a fantastic idea. Eating dinner together allowed us to vent about our days, refuel our bodies, and relax and bond with each other before talking about our goals. Once we started running out of things to talk about during dinner, I decided that this was actually a great time to bring up our family vision.

"As you all know, we're going to have our meeting after dinner. Before we do that though, I'd love for us to agree on something," I announced. "Ella and Lexi, you don't know about this yet, but your mom and I actually created a vision statement for our family. Do you know what a vision statement is?" I asked.

"Is it like a plan?" Lexi responded.

"Sort of! It's more like the outcome of a plan. A vision statement defines what matters most to all of us and where we to end up. If we have a family vision statement and consider it often, we will be more likely to stay aligned with it and eventually achieve it. In other words, having a family vision statement will make us more successful."

"So then what's our family vision statement?" Ella asked.

"Well your mom and I created one, but we want your guys' opinions on it. If we want our family vision statement to make all of us happy, we all need to agree on it," I explained. Next, I read the family vision statement out loud and waited for Ella and Lexi to respond.

"That sounds good to me!" Lexi replied.

"Me too!" Ella added.

I didn't want them to just accept it though, I wanted them to challenge it and contribute to it! I wasn't just going to let them go that easy.

"Okay, well I appreciate that, but I'd love some more input. If you had to change something about it, what would you change? Or is there anything you would add?"

"Well I mean, it doesn't say anything about having fun," Lexi mentioned. "Could we add something about that, maybe?"

She was totally right. I didn't even realize that the vision statement didn't say to have fun! And considering how many of our goals fell under the Pleasure category, it probably should.

"That's a great point, Lexi," I replied. "Does everyone agree that the word 'fun' should be in our vision statement?"

"Yeah!" Rachel and Ella responded.

"Okay, but before I make that update, is there anything else we want to change about it? Ella, do you have anything you'd like to modify or add?"

"Um … Well, it doesn't say anything about spending time together. And I thought we were going to get more time with you!" Ella explained.

"That's another great point … Okay, how about I just add one more sentence then! It could say something like, 'We will also spend a lot more quality time together and have a lot of fun whenever we do.'"

"That's perfect!" Ella replied.

"Great! Lexi and Rachel, what do you think?"

"I think we just nailed it on the head," Rachel replied.

"I agree!" Lexi added.

Once everyone concluded that our finally vision statement was now perfect, I made a mental note to add it to the goals spreadsheet after dinner. That way, at the beginning of every family meeting, we would see and remember it.

If you're concerned that your family won't enjoy the meeting, I suggest that you have a family dinner first too. You could also do something else together, like going on a walk or going out for ice cream. The point is to do something that will give everyone a chance to relax, refuel and bond. This way, everyone will be more positive and prepared for the meeting.

I also suggest that you talk about your family vision before the meeting like I did. Just present the vision you currently have and ask everyone for feedback. Do they feel like it accurately reflects what everyone in your family wants? Is there anything they want to change or add? Is there anything they want to remove? Having this conversation at dinner will help everyone get on the same page and envision the end goal before the first family meeting begins.

Once my family and I were done with dinner, we gathered in our family room. "Before we begin, let's remind ourselves what this family meeting is for," I announced. "On the retreat we had a few weeks ago, we all decided what goals and plans we wanted to achieve this year. Now that it's been a few weeks and we've had some time to process everything, we're going to revisit the goals and make sure that we still agree with them."

"Why wouldn't we still agree with them?" Rachel asked.

"Well, there could be a chance that while we were on the retreat, we became too eager and ambitious with our goals. This meeting will help us ensure that we weren't being too ridiculous, and will give us the chance to adjust our goals if necessary."

"Ahh, okay, that makes sense," Rachel replied.

"We'll also talk about what the next steps are for each goal so that we can start making progress on them! Does that sound like a plan?" Everyone nodded.

"Great! To make this meeting easier for us, I created a Google spreadsheet that lists all of our goals. We each have our own tab, and the goals that we are responsible for are listed in our tabs," I explained. As I was saying this, I connected my laptop to our television screen so that everyone could see the spreadsheet.

"Since my tab is the first one on here, we can just go through my goals first," I decided. "The first goal on mine is family game night!"

"We already decided that we're going to have a family game night once a month. Is everyone still okay with that?"

"Yeah!" Rachel and Ella replied. Lexi remained silent.

"Lexi, what's wrong?" I asked.

"I mean, I'd love to have more than one a month," she explained. I wanted to respect her wish to have them more often, but I knew that with all of the other goals, we might not have the time. And I definitely didn't want to overextend ourselves right away.

"Okay, how about this... We'll leave the goal at once a month for now, but if in a few months we all agree that the game nights can happen more often, we can upgrade to twice a month. And don't forget—we can always have spontaneous game nights too," I tried to reason.

"Okay, I like that!" Lexi replied.

"Great! So let's decide when we want to have our first family game night then. Let me pull up my calendar," I said. I was referring to my Google Calendar, which contains all of my personal and work events. I absolutely love this calendar because it helps me stay organized and remember everything I have going on. It also lets my family and co-workers see when I'm busy and when I'm free. I even use it to plan out what time and day I will complete certain work tasks, which is why I consider it to be my ultimate time management tool.

"It looks like I have most Friday nights free. How about you guys?" I asked.

"Yeah, we're all usually free on Friday nights," Rachel replied. She is the one who usually keeps track of Ella's and Lexi's schedules, so I knew I could trust her input.

"Great, then let's shoot for the Friday two weeks from now," I concluded.

As we went through the next goals, the Google Calendar really came in handy. For instance, another goal of mine was to have two date nights with Rachel every month. Thanks to the calendar, we were able to plan and schedule out our first two date nights. During your family meeting, I definitely recommend that you use a Calendar tool such as Google Calendar. Doing so will help everyone keep track of their goals, manage their time, and ultimately be more successful. If you aren't familiar with Google Calendar or if your family isn't tech-savvy, you can use a printed calendar instead.

After we finished talking through my goals, we went to Ella's tab on the Google spreadsheet to discuss hers. Ella was still happy with how much time she committed to each goal, so we spent most of the time clarifying and calendaring her next steps. We also discussed some of her goals more thoroughly so that she could better understand what they entailed. For example, during the Dream Board presentations, Ella mentioned that one of her goals was to improve her relationship with Lexi. Lexi agreed to do something fun with Ella at least once a week to help her achieve this goal. However, Ella and Lexi never discussed what they would do together, so I figured this was a perfect opportunity to bring it up.

"I know that you and Lexi are going to hang out once a week, but what kind of things do you want to do together?" I asked.

"Well, I don't know... Just like, sister stuff!" she replied. "Like paint our nails, and stay up late talking."

"Those are good ideas! But if you stay up too late talking, you'll both be cranky the next day and the fighting definitely won't stop then. So let's think of some other things you can do. Lexi, what do you think? What would you like to do with your sister?"

"Hmm ... I *do* love painting my nails. It's also really fun when we watch movies in my room together. Maybe we could have more movie nights!" Lexi exclaimed.

"Yeah I love those too!" Ella agreed.

"Great! We'll make sure you get more movie nights together then. How about we put one on the calendar right now?"

"Yeah!" they both agreed.

"Okay well it should probably be on a weekend night because you have a later bedtime on those nights. And ideally, it should be on a weekend when we don't have a bunch of other stuff going on."

I glanced over the calendar and found one Saturday that looked pretty free. "How about this Saturday here?" I suggested.

"Works for me!" Ella and Lexi both responded.

After we finished going through Ella's goals, we moved onto Lexi's tab on the spreadsheet. We ended up modifying a couple of her goals to make them more specific. For instance, one of Lexi's goals was to make more friends, but we struggled to determine the best way she could do this during the retreat. We decided to refine this goal of hers at a later time when we had more ideas. Once we remembered this during the first family meeting, we started doing some research and throwing ideas around. At one point, Rachel mentioned that Lexi could join Girl Scouts to make new friends. Lexi absolutely loved that idea, so she agreed to research Girl Scouts groups to join before the next meeting.

Once we got to the end of Lexi's spreadsheet, I asked her if there was anything else she wanted to change or add. The second I finished saying this, she started bouncing up and down in her seat.

"Oh my god, that reminds me!" Lexi responded excitedly. "I totally forgot to bring something up when I was presenting my dream board. Am I allowed to add another goal?"

"Of course!" I replied.

"Great! Because I thought it would be fun if I could hang out with everyone alone more. Like you know, just us two," she explained. "Daddy, you and I could go out to dinner sometime. And Mommy, we could go shopping or something! Then Ella and I can have more movie nights like we talked about."

"I would love that, Lexi!" Rachel replied. "What a great idea. What made you think of that?"

"Well, Daddy and I hung out just us two a couple months ago, and it was really fun!"

"What did you like about it?" Rachel asked curiously.

"We got dinner just the two of us, and he let me decide where we went. He also took me to get ice cream after dinner, even though he couldn't have any because he's allergic. I thought that was really nice of him, and I had a great night. I was hoping we could do more stuff like that," Lexi explained.

I knew exactly which night she was referring to, and we really did have a great time. We were getting along really well and laughing all night, and she opened up to me quite a bit. I hadn't seen that side of her in a while. I remember after that night, I told myself to spend more one-on-one time with her whenever I got the chance. But unfortunately, it just slipped my mind.

"Lexi, I had a blast that night too, and I'm sorry we haven't hung out just us two since then," I said. "But I can add it to our goals spreadsheets so that we can remember to make it happen."

Then I turned to Ella. "Ella, would you like more one-on-one time with me and Mom too?"

"Yeah! That sounds like a lot of fun!" she replied.

"Okay then, so how about once every other week, I'll go out with Lexi and Mommy will go out with Ella?" I suggested. "Then the next time, we can switch!" Everyone loved the idea, so we scheduled our first one-on-one parent daughter hangouts on the Google Calendar.

****

"IF IT WASN'T FOR THIS ROADMAP, I WOULD HAVE NEVER KNOWN THAT MY DAUGHTERS (AND MY WIFE) WANTED MORE ONE-ON-ONE TIME WITH ME AND ONE ANOTHER."

****

If it wasn't for this roadmap, I would have never known that my daughters (and my wife) wanted more one-on-one time with me and one another. I always thought that all of us spending time together as a family was just as effective and valuable than spending time together one-on-one, so I never really prioritized it. But once I really thought about it, I realized how ignorant it was for me think this way. Literally every day at StringCan, I'm reminded about the value of one-on-one communication.

At StringCan, I meet one-on-one with each manager for at least fifteen minutes once a week. Once I first started doing these meetings, I couldn't believe how much better I understood and connected with my team members. It became quickly obvious to me that they were much more open and transparent when it was just us two in the room. They would share more of their personal opinions, they would voice concerns when they had them, and they would share more personal stories about what was going on in their lives. These one-on-one meetings were more insightful and valuable than I could have ever initially imagined.

I knew there were a few different reasons why one-on-one meetings were so effective. First, when our entire team is together, my attention is being divided up among multiple people. This makes it nearly impossible to really understand and deeply connect with every person, which prevents me from establishing a meaningful relationship with each of them. Also, conversations tend to be more surface-level when we are all together, which causes important conversations to be pushed to the side. If I really want to connect with my co-workers and really know what's on their minds, one-on-one meetings are essential.

In reality, this same logic applies to your friends and family. If you spend more one-on-one time with those who are important to you, it's really likely that you will have more meaningful conversations and establish a deeper connection with them. It's just easier to open up and be honest when less people are around. If you want to strengthen your relationship with each of your family members, make more one-on-one time one of your goals too. I can almost guarantee that you aren't the only one who wants it.

***

By the time we got to Rachel's tab on the spreadsheet, our Google Calendar had a lot going on. As a result, we had to adjust things a couple times to accommodate all our goals and schedules. For example, one of Rachel's goals was to attend Weight Watchers every Thursday night. But because we hadn't put this on the calendar yet, we already had some of our one-on-ones scheduled for Thursday nights. Fortunately, it really wasn't an issue to move them to other nights. We just had to get creative and push certain plans out a little farther.

We had to modify our calendar like this quite a few times during the meeting, but we didn't let it bother us. It honestly felt like a puzzle or a game; we had to figure out how all of our different plans and goals best fit together. We stayed positive and determined to create a schedule that worked, and eventually we accomplished just that. When our calendar was finally complete, it was amazing and exciting to see all of our goals mapped out together. It felt like we had just found out how to balance everything that mattered in our lives, which was the whole point of the retreat.

As you go through everyone's goals and putting things on the calendar, there's a good chance you'll run into this situation too. At some point, your goals and plans may conflict. When this happens, just remember that you can always adjust events you already put on the Google Calendar. You can adjust events on a printed calendar too, as long as you use a pencil!

Also keep in mind that you have an *entire year* to complete these goals! You don't necessarily need to make progress on all of them before the next meeting. As long as you make some sort of progress on at least your most important goals, you will probably be able to stay on track. Don't be too hard on yourself or your family, and don't overload your calendar too much. You don't want the calendar to stress anyone out, so make sure everyone is okay with the events you're calendaring. Also make sure to save plenty of time for rest and relaxation.

Once you are done talking about your goals and creating your calendar, discuss when the next family meeting will be. Let them know that this first family meeting was longer because we had to map the upcoming goals on the calendar. Now that the calendaring is complete, we can just review progress at future meetings and just make edits to the calendar. Also remind everyone that they are expected to make progress on their goals by the time that next meeting comes around. Then finally, make sure that you ask everyone to hold one another accountable for these goals. You'll definitely need accountability if you want everyone to be successful.

***

ACCOUNTABILITY IN ACTION

After our first meeting, I was really excited and determined to commit to my goals. It was like starting a new project that I was extremely passionate about. Of course, the first few weeks worked out really well for me! I made my family and my goals a top priority so that I could stay true to my word.

As I shared in the prior chapter, after a few weeks went by, I started slipping up. Business at StringCan was really starting to take off, so I had more business events and meetings than I've ever experienced in my life. As a result, I fell behind on some of my goals. I stopped going to the gym three times a week, and I wasn't maintaining a healthy diet. Sure, I was still dedicating a lot more time to my family, but I was sacrificing my personal health. I was very aware of this, but I just didn't really see any other option.

Eventually, Rachel drew attention to it. But the way she did it was quite sneaky and very smart. One day when I was coming home from a really stressful day at work, I called Rachel and almost immediately started venting about my day. I'm sure she could tell that I was clearly anxious and uptight. Eventually when I stopped talking to take a breath, she responded.

"Well I'm sorry you had such a rough day. Maybe you should stop by the gym on your way home so you can let out all of your frustration," she recommended. I knew she probably suggested the gym because it had been weeks since I had gone, but she made a pretty good point. If I went to the gym before I went home, I could get some exercise while also distressing from the day. This way, I could be in a much better state of mind when I got home.

Before, I always thought of the gym as just *more work*. I also feel selfish for going because it takes away time from me being with my family. But then Rachel framed the gym in an entirely new way for me. When I realized that the gym could help me de-stress before going home, I saw new value in it that I didn't consider before. In addition to working on my personal health goals, going to the gym could help me be a happier father and husband. When I thought about it like that, it became much more appealing to me.

A few weeks later, Rachel persuaded me to eat better too. We were just relaxing at home one night when she started casually talking about her health and fitness goals.

"I still really want to lose about ten more pounds," Rachel explained. I agreed that I wanted to do the same. Then she said, "Hey, what if we made it a competition?"

A competition? That definitely piqued my interest. I'm a very competitive person, and I love winning, so it was a pretty great idea. If we made this a competition, I would definitely be more motivated to work out and eat healthier. Once I told her I was interested, we discussed what our wagers would be. If Rachel won, then I agreed to clean up the kitchen after every meal for the week. If I won, Rachel said she would wash my car by hand.

Ever since I had those conversations with Rachel, I've been much better about going to the gym and watching what I eat. I won't lie, I'm far from perfect, but committing to my personal health goals is much easier now and I feel much more motivated to follow through on them.

If you want to hold you family accountable for their goals, focus on motivating them rather than pestering them. Don't call them out on what they *aren't* doing—just remind them what it is they *want to be* doing. If you're worried about coming across as judgmental or annoying, I recommend using one of Rachel's techniques. Try framing the goal differently by explaining what other benefits it will provide—or create a competition around the goal. What can you offer as a reward if they complete the goal? Or what consequences will they face if they don't? If you make the goal more significant or intriguing, you can help your family members more willingly commit to them.

However, no matter how you choose to hold your family members accountable, it's extremely important that you use the right tone and voice. If you sound pushy, disappointed and/or frustrated, you will make your family members feel like they are already failing. As a result, they will only become *less encouraged* to work toward their goals. They may also get upset that you are showing little faith and being really hard on them, which can lead to arguments.

Instead of expressing negative attitudes, express love, hopefulness and enthusiasm. Let your family members know that they have what it takes to accomplish their goals, but they need to take the next steps. Emphasize that if they take the next steps, it will be completely worth it. Get them excited to pursue their goals, and tell them that you have faith in them.

Now, I realize there may be times when you feel *very* disappointed or frustrated with your family. For instance, if it's been months since somebody made progress on their goals, being sincere and loving may feel impossible. Thankfully, there are ways to overcome this. First, write out how you're feeling. Explain how frustrated you are, why you're feeling frustrated, and what would make you less frustrated. Vent as much as you need until you attain some peace of mind. This will help you relieve some tension and remain calm when talking to this family member. Next, focus on the positives and remember what you're grateful for. What is going right? What are you proud of? Keep the answers to these questions top of mind before confronting the family member.

Here are some other accountability Dos and Don'ts

Do:

1. Occasionally ask everyone how they are doing on their goals (e.g. every other Wednesday)
2. Mention specific goals in casual conversation when appropriate
3. Offer your time and/or assistance whenever possible
4. Be patient; change takes time
5. Acknowledge and praise anyone who is working on their goals

Don't:

1. Ask everyone how they are doing on their goals every day
2. Be passive aggressive when mentioning goals in casual conversation
3. Guilt-trip the family member into working on their goals
4. Rudely point out when they aren't completing their goals
5. Tempt them to put off or go against their goals (e.g. eating unhealthy food)

If a family member ever responds negatively to you holding them accountable, explain that you are only trying to help. Apologize if you've upset them, and ask what you can do differently to more effectively motivate them. View it as a learning opportunity; find out what your family members truly need to achieve their goals.

DISCUSSING PROGRESS

Ever since our second annual retreat ended, my family and I have been very diligent about meeting once a month to discuss our progress on our goals. These meetings definitely help us stay on the right track, but that's not the only purpose they serve. In fact, I think the real benefit of these meetings is that they reinforce everything we learned on the retreat. It's almost as if we get to relive the retreat once every month, which I am incredibly thankful for. As a result, the retreat's influence on my family is still very apparent and continues to grow stronger with time.

These meetings also serve as a perfect time to complete one of our family goals: talking about respect and communication once a month. At the beginning of every meeting, I ask everyone to acknowledge at least one family member for saying or doing something respectful in the past month. For example, one time Ella mentioned that Lexi let her borrow one of her favorite dolls. Ella thanked Lexi once again for sharing her doll, and Rachel and I told Lexi that we were proud of her for sharing her toys. I feel like this tradition. has encouraged us to not only respect each other more, but to also notice respectful behaviors

****

"THIS TRADITION HAS ENCOURAGED US TO NOT ONLY RESPECT EACH OTHER MORE, BUT TO ALSO NOTICE RESPECTFUL BEHAVIORS MORE."

****

more. Plus, it's always such a positive way to start our meetings. I strongly recommend that your family does the same. I got this idea from my team at StringCan. At our monthly team meetings, we start out with Recognizing the Wins and team members have the chance to talk about a team member who has gone above and beyond or celebrating a win we had as a group. Starting our meetings off with this kind of positive communication sets a great tone for the rest of the meeting.

Once we complete the family recognition task, we pull up the goals spreadsheet and each take turns going through our goals. We explain the progress we've made on each of our goals and confirm whether or not we need any additional support. When it's clear that we've successfully made progress on a goal, everyone cheers and congratulates the goal owner. And thanks to the new level of support and empowerment within our home, this happens all the time during our meetings.

In fact, ever since we started using this roadmap, we've been accomplishing all sorts of things. For example, Ella is getting better grades in school and Lexi is making new friends. I can tell their levels of self-confidence are skyrocketing, and that's really impressive for girls their age. They are noticeably more driven and determined to do their best, and they have no doubt in their minds that they can't achieve any realistic goal they set for themselves. Aside from their mindsets, their behavior has significantly improved too. Of course, they still bicker most days; however, they are much more respectful toward us and others.

As far as Rachel's new accomplishments, she is finally doing more of the things that she loves. She is volunteering more, started a new business, taking cooking classes, and attending a monthly book club with her closest friends. Considering that she spends most of her time working, and taking care of me and the girls, we are all really excited that she is making more time for herself. Because she's relaxing and enjoying herself more often, she is much more vibrant and positive. Don't get me wrong, she was always enjoyable to be around—unless of course, I messed something up and pissed her off. But now, she seems truly happy and is a lot more calm when one of us doesn't do something right.

Then of course, there's me. I've committed to most of my goals, which I couldn't be more excited about. I'm mostly proud that I'm using my smoker more often and spending more quality time with my family. I can't even explain how much joy and fulfillment that these two simple goals have given me. They remind me to stop working and enjoy what life is really about, which is dramatically enhancing my quality of life. I'm also really happy that I'm reading more books and going to the gym on a regular basis. These are two things that I've been meaning to do for years, but I just kept pushing them off. Now instead of daydreaming about them, I'm actually doing them! I finally have the time to make these two activities happen because I finally figured out how to balance my life goals and priorities. As a result, I have significantly boosted my self confidence and personal health, which are two things I often lacked in the past.

In order to achieve all these goals, I've been spending less time working. But believe it or not, working less hasn't negatively impacted my career whatsoever. Ironically enough, business has taken off every since I stopped obsessing over work. Sure, it could just be a coincidence, but I highly doubt it. Now that I'm taking better care of my family and myself, I've noticed that I'm in a much better state of mind when I'm at work. I'm able to think more clearly as a result, which is allowing me to make better decisions and develop smarter solutions. I also believe that ever since my family and I went on the retreat, I've been a lot more positive and likeable as a person. This could explain why I'm getting along better with employees at work—and why I'm attracting more clients. Needless to say, spending more time on myself and my family is actually benefiting my career.

ADDRESSING UNACCEPTABLE EXCUSES

Sometimes, even if a goal is very reasonable and beneficial, someone in our family still fails to follow through with it. This typically happens because unexpected things come up, such as urgent business trips or a big school test. As a result, we aren't able to make progress on or complete all of our goals every month. And really, that's okay! That's just how life goes sometimes. We can't be perfect, and we can't predict what's going to happen in life. If you or another family member occasionally misses the mark because of unforeseen circumstances, don't get frustrated or disappointed. Just push yourself or the family member to dedicate more time to this goal moving forward.

However, every once in awhile, somebody doesn't complete one of their goals even though nothing unexpected came up that month. When this is the case, we don't just let it slide and move on. Instead, we get a little confrontational and dig deeper. We ask the goal owner, "Why weren't you able to this goal?" And we pinpoint what is getting in the way. More often than not, our reasons and excuses are really weak.

One time during a family meeting, we were discussing Ella's goal of reading at least 20 minutes a night. When I asked her how she was doing on this goal, she admitted that she had barely read all month. Then Rachel asked her why this was happening in order to determine a solution.

"I really hate reading and I just don't want to do it," she bluntly stated.

This response didn't surprise me, but I knew it wasn't an acceptable excuse.

"Ella, we all have to do things we don't like sometimes. But if we do them, we will be much happier and successful later on," I explained. "Do you remember why you made reading more a goal in the first place?"

"Well I decided that reading could make me a better speller and writer—and I want to be less afraid to read out loud in class," Ella recalled.

"When you aren't feeling motivated to read, why don't you try to recall how much you want those results? That way, you'll remember why you want to read and you will be more willing to do it!" I explained.

"I guess that's true! Yeah, I think that will really help," Ella responded.

If your family members ever explain that they just aren't motivated enough to commit to one of their goals, remind them why they established the goal in the first place. Encourage them to focus on the long-term results, and explain how rewarding it will be if they remain diligent and disciplined. This way, they will be more willing to stick with it.

You can also mention some of the negative outcomes they will face if they don't complete their goals, such as personal unfulfillment and disappointment. However, it's much more effective to be encouraging rather than threatening. And being supportive is exceptionally helpful. Ask your family member what you can do to help them stick to their goal. For example, maybe you can remind them about it more or work on the goal with them. Either way, just be as loving and helpful as you can so that you can help your family be successful.

Another excuse you may hear is "I just don't have enough time." As you've probably figured out by now, I hate this excuse more than anything. When people say this, here is what I really hear: "I chose to prioritize other things." Because when something matters to us, *we make time for it*. Whether that means spending a little less time on another important project or sacrificing some shut-eye, we always find a way. When we say, "I just don't have enough time," the real problem is that we just don't care enough.

With that being said, we don't even really need *more time* to accomplish *more goals*. We just need to commit to managing our time more wisely. If you or another family member is struggling with time management, help each other out. Walk each other through your days or weekly schedules, and try to identify habits that can be changed in order to free up more time. For instance, could your son take advantage of his long drive to work? Or could your spouse make dinner once a week, instead of every day? Focus on the small yet time-consuming aspects of each day.

Here are some of my personal and favorite time management tips:

1. Plan out your days ahead of time.
2. As soon as you wake up, complete your three important tasks of the day (before you go to work or school).
3. Maintain an updated to-do list in your phone and reference it whenever you have free time.
4. Take advantage of idle time (e.g. respond to emails while you're waiting at the doctor's office).
5. Outsource time-consuming tasks (e.g. bookkeeping, cleaning, grocery shopping).
6. Stop watching television.
7. Limit time on social media.
8. Turn down invitations to plans that don't benefit you.
9. Get errands done on your lunch break.

You may also hear the "it's not my priority" excuse, which is similar to the "no time" excuse. If you or another family member decides that certain goals are less important than others, you will inevitably decide that it's okay to dedicate less time to those goals. However, just because some goals are less important than others *individually*, they are all equally important *collectively*.

You created goals for every category that matters to you, which means that committing to all of your goals will help you maintain a well-balanced lifestyle. If you make certain goals less important than others, and you habitually run out of time to complete them, you won't be able to maintain a well-balanced lifestyle. Don't prioritize your goals; *balance* them. Fortunately, managing your time more effectively will help you achieve this as well.

MODIFYING YOUR GOALS

One time during one of my family meetings, we were discussing our goal to have more family game nights. At first, we were doing a great job with this goal! We were having family game nights every month just like we had planned, and they were usually a great time. But after a few months of this tradition, they sort of just stopped happening. We all started to ignore the calendar reminders, and nobody brought up the topic. But when we had our next family meeting, we were forced to talk about it.

"The next goal on my list is the family game nights, which are supposed to happen once a month," I began. "Obviously, this hasn't been the case lately. And I feel like we've all been avoiding talking about it. I would like to discuss this more. How does everyone feel about the family game nights? Lexi, what are your thoughts?" I asked.

"I mean I usually love them, but I feel like the last few game nights we've had weren't as fun as they used to be. They are starting to get boring since we do them so much. That's why I haven't cared that they haven't been happening lately," Lexi explained.

"Does everyone agree with that?" I asked. Everyone nodded.

"Why haven't they been as fun as they used to be?" I continued.

"I think it's because we've been trying to do them too often," Rachel responded. "It just feels really forced, and it's not a special occasion anymore."

"I completely agree, Rachel," I replied. "Maybe once a month wasn't the right move for us. I think if we had the family game nights once a quarter instead, we would be more likely to make them happen and we would enjoy them a lot more," I explained. "What does everyone think? Should we modify the goal?" Fortunately, everyone nodded.

As time goes on, you may also come across goals that are suddenly no longer being met. Certain goals won't actually be as realistic or beneficial as you initially thought they would be, and your priorities may change. Realize that it's okay if you need to modify or even remove goals later on. These goals are supposed to make your family happier and stronger, so if you realize they aren't accomplishing that mission anymore, don't be afraid to make some adjustments.

If you think about it, this is a scenario that happens all the time in business. While it's essential to create an initial strategy and solid goals for your business, your strategy and goals will need to adapt and change as time goes on. For example, if you realize a certain process isn't working anymore, you need to change the process so that your business can be more efficient and successful. Otherwise, you would just keep using a process that isn't benefitting your business—and we both know that's just dumb.

STICKING WITH IT

Because we've had so much success with this roadmap, my family and I decided to make the Family 2.0 Roadmap an annual family tradition. We really enjoyed it the first time around and gained so much from the experience, so why would we not do it again? The entire roadmap allowed us to grow closer as a family and achieve new things. I would love for these two things to happen every year!

We used the roadmap again and it was even better the second time around. In the first retreat, respect was a popular topic. In the second retreat, spending and saving money needed to be a focus. Everyone was already clear on how the retreat would be structured and all the same activities took a lot less time to complete. This gave us the extra time needed to inject new activities. We kicked off the second annual retreat by reading the letters and presented the new additional topic around money.

Over the prior year, our kids started earning allowance each week and we noticed that they were wasting money on toys that ended up getting donated a few months later. What was a bigger concern to me is that they did not seem to grasp the concept of saving. We were getting frustrated by this and decided we would tackle this at our next family retreat. To make sure our kids understand the value of a dollar, we created a new exercise to have our daughters guess how much their favorite items or experiences cost. We created a poster that had pictures of their favorite restaurants, toys, vacations and transportation. The items that were lower cost under $300 they guessed the amounts pretty close; however, the larger items they were very far off. For example, both Lexi and Ella guessed the cost of an iWatch within $100; however, they guessed Rachel's new car was only $5,000 and they were off by about $45,000. It was definitely an eye opening experience for all of us.

Once we decided our daughters better grasped the value of a dollar, we then announced a new money management plan. I got this idea from another EO member, Luke Ford, who is the founder of My Computer Works. We told our kids that from now on they could buy whatever they want, within reason. They were so excited and after a few seconds looked at us with a "what's the catch" face. We told them that they were going to start earning money each month, similar to how employees at my company work, as long as they do their family job (e.g. chores).

When we get home, I told them we will go to the bank and open their own bank account with the money they have saved plus their monthly family pay of $50 each. Then each month we would continue to give them their "salary" of $50/month. Each week we will review their bank account and determine how much money they have, what items they want to buy and how long it would take to save up for it. We also talked about the concept of need vs. want and this helped them understand what we would buy for

****

"TO TEACH THEM THE CONCEPT OF SAVING, WE OFFERED THEM AN INCENTIVE THAT EVERY THREE MONTHS WE WOULD LOOK AT THE BALANCE AND PAY THEM AN ADDITIONAL 10% ON THEIR BALANCE."

****

them vs. what they need to buy. The items that were essential such as clothes for school or family meals we would cover those costs. Any item that they want but don't need would be up to their discretion, as long as it was age appropriate.

To teach them the concept of saving, we offered them an incentive that every three months we would look at the balance on their account and pay them an additional 10% on their savings balance. We spent some time showing them how this would work and the benefit over the year that the more they saved the more they would earn. They understood this a lot better than we expected, as long as we continued to explain it in a child friendly way. For example, Lexi loves American Girl dolls where they can cost around $100 a doll. If she wanted to buy a new iPad we told her that would equal five or more American Girl dolls.

This new concept over the past few months is already working great as our kids have significantly reduced asking us for silly toys and they are excited about saving each month. I love that my young daughters over the next few years will gain financial knowledge that will prepare them for adulthood, especially college. I encourage you to talk with your spouse each year and decide on a theme or challenge you want to focus on each year. At your annual family retreat you can create specific exercises around those topics to encourage improved communication and resolution.

The main benefit of following this roadmap every year is that it reinforces everything you learned or gained the first time around. Whether you attained certain values, insights, or techniques from your retreat, attending the retreat every year will allow you to remember and reflect on them. And sadly, it's really easy for us to forget how to effectively communicate and respect each other. It's just human nature to need reminders.

Here are some other benefits that you'll gain from adopting this annual tradition:

1. **Family bonding time.** This roadmap allows you to spend more quality time with your family and have more meaningful conversations with each other.
2. **Transparency.** The retreat is one of the safest times and places to be completely honest with each other.
3. **Alignment.** The conversations that this roadmap initiates ensure that everyone continues to get along and stay on the same page.
4. **Clarity.** Having these conversations every year will help everyone remember who they are, where they want to go, and what matters most them.
5. **Life fulfillment.** This roadmap helps you achieve your goals and dreams so that you and everyone in your family can live a happier, more fulfilling life.
6. **Flexibility.** Over time, our goals and dreams can change. Following this roadmap every year will allow you to establish new goals and dreams.
7. **Empowerment.** Family traditions increase our sense of belonging and stability, which helps us feel more comfortable and confident.

Also, remember that people change over time. Our wants and needs don't always stay the same, and we often modify our personal goals and dreams. This is especially true for children who are still growing and finding themselves. In fact, there's a good chance that their thoughts and life perspectives will change at least somewhat every year. By going on the retreat once a year, you can find out how everyone has changed and where they currently stand. Then you can adjust your goals and plans accordingly to ensure they still empower everyone to be happy and successful. You can also establish new goals and plans that better align with where everyone is currently at. This way, your plans and goals for each year will be relevant and unique.

THINGS TO KEEP IN MIND

Now that I've successfully followed this roadmap with my family two times, I've spent a lot of time reflecting back on how it all went. I've also shared my experience with well over 250 friends and colleagues, and I've encouraged them to experience it too. After our first retreat, I was explaining this roadmap to a friend, he asked a *really* great question. He said, "If you were to do it all over again, would you have done anything differently?" Nobody had asked me that, and I never considered it myself. My mind went blank, I wasn't able to answer him. I told him to give me some time to think about it.

WHAT I WOULD HAVE DONE DIFFERENTLY

Well, I thought about it and yes, there are a few things I would have changed and did with our second retreat. While I don't have any regrets as to how everything played out, I feel like there are a few things I could have done to make the entire roadmap more beneficial for myself and my family the first time around.

Let's start with the actual family retreat. As you probably realized, I ended up facilitating most of the *entire* first retreat. I'm not saying that with pride, I'm saying that with exasperation. I was always telling everyone what we were going to do and how we were going to do it. I also had to constantly encourage everyone else to talk. I struggled to contribute my own opinions and ideas because I was too busy trying to support and encourage everyone else. I also felt like I was controlling everything and being "bossy" in a sense, which just didn't feel great. Although my family never complained about this, I still didn't like it.

During the retreat, I felt like there was nothing I could do about this problem. I was the only one who understood how the roadmap really worked, so I felt like I had to explain everything and guide everyone through it. I also thought I needed to control the order of the presentations and how much time we spent on everything to ensure that each day went smoothly. A few months after the retreat, I began to consider what I could have done differently to avoid always being in charge. Eventually I realized that I had this same problem at StringCan when the business was in its early stages. I falsely believed that because I was the CEO, it was my responsibility to lead everything. Whether it was a meeting, discussion, team building activity or a new project, I just presumed that everyone expected and needed me to take charge.

I assumed the lead at work for years until finally, some of my team members spoke up. They expressed that they wanted to take on more responsibilities and be in charge of more projects, which would include leading many of our meetings. I couldn't believe I didn't consider or encourage this sooner. Being in charge all the time exhausted me, but I didn't think anyone else was willing to do it. When I heard my employees tell me that they wanted to step up, I was relieved. Now I put them in charge a lot more often and it's worked out wonderfully. Whenever I get to act as a participant rather than a facilitator, I'm able to be a lot more present and contribute more ideas. As for my team members, they get to practice their leadership skills more often and become more comfortable speaking in front of others. It's just a win-win all around!

After I reflected on this, I realized I could have asked my family to take the lead every once in awhile during the retreat. At the very least, I could have asked Rachel for more help. She is perfectly capable of giving instructions and leading discussions, so I probably could have put her in charge of certain activities. For example, I could have walked us through the reflection board activity and she could have facilitated the dream board activity. As long as she understood the instructions and goals for the activity we were doing, I don't see why this wouldn't have worked. And really, the same applies to Ella and Lexi. I certainly could have put them in charge of the easier activities, such as reviewing the timeline or toy box. They may have struggled a bit to say all the right things, but it would have given them the opportunity to practice their leadership and public speaking skills. It also would have taken a lot of the pressure and attention off of me. On our second retreat, we tested this out and Rachel facilitated about 50% of the exercises and I found that to be very beneficial.

Also, when we *weren't* completing activities, I really didn't need to be in charge of what was happening. I could have asked Rachel or one of the girls, "What we do the rest of the day is entirely up to you!" Or I could have put them in charge of something specific, like dinner or a game of charades. This way, they wouldn't have felt like I was always telling them what to do. Everyone would have gotten a chance to be in control at one point or another, and I would have gotten to participate more.

If you get really tired of facilitating everything during the retreat, don't be afraid to put someone else in charge for a bit. Especially if you feel like a certain family member is sick of listening to you, tell them to take over. This will ensure that everyone stays engaged and you don't wear yourself out. If your children are too young to lead activities or discussions, ask your spouse to split up the workload with you. I would suggest that you lead the first two days, and she leads the second two.

During the retreat, I also wish I would have encouraged everyone to give each other more shoutouts, recognition and praise. As mentioned earlier, at StringCan, we call these "kudos." Every time we start certain meetings, such as quarterly team meetings, I ask, "Does anyone want to give out any kudos?" Normally, there's at least one person who has something to say. We often give each other kudos for completing big projects, solving problems, brainstorming great ideas, and meeting deadlines. We give out kudos for small and trivial things too, like if someone made us all laugh one day or brought in donuts one morning. It's just a fun way to show our appreciation for each other, and it helps everyone remember that they are valued. Also, because we all love getting kudos, it motivates us to work harder and help each other out more.

If I considered how beneficial kudos could be on the retreat before it happened, I'm sure I would have encouraged them all the time. Kudos are major mood-boosters, and they make everyone feel more loved and appreciated. If we gave each other kudos at the beginning of every conversation on the retreat, all of our talks would have started out on a very positive note. For that reason, kudos are a perfect substitute for the Achievements worksheet on the first night. Sadly though, I didn't realize this until after the retreat. We didn't end up give each other kudos *or* completing the Achievements worksheet! We obviously still managed without either of them, but

I feel like recognizing each other more would have really enhanced our experience.

If you want to ensure that the retreat is a really positive and loving time for your family, I definitely encourage you to give each other kudos. You could start by giving an example, such as: "I really want to give your mom some praise for making us all lunch today. That was really nice of her, and it was delicious!" After everyone agrees and thanks her, you could say, "Does someone want to give anyone else kudos for something they did today?" If nobody has anything to contribute, let them know there will be more opportunities to give kudos. You also might want to say something like this: "I bet if we start paying more attention to the small, positive things that all of us are doing, we'll all want to give out kudos next time."

The last change I would have made to the retreat would be the goals we established. We came up with dozens of goals, and it's really exciting that we're following through with many of them. However, I would be lying if I said committing to all these goals has been fun and easy. It's definitely a lot of hard work, and it really stresses me out sometimes. Sometimes I wish we would have chosen fewer and more conservative goals. After all, the whole point of this roadmap isn't to improve and accomplish as much as possible within a year. The point is to strengthen our family, which only requires taking a few more steps in the right direction. This relates one of my favorite analogies: "How do you eat an elephant? One bite at a time."

If I were you, I'd focus on taking baby steps and go for some easy wins first. Establish goals that you and your family can easily follow through on, and don't be overly ambitious. If you solely focus on making small improvements, your family will be more successful and the roadmap will also be a thousand times more enjoyable. You'll also avoid overwhelming yourself and your family members with dozens of new, intimidating goals. For example, if a family member says they want to learn to speak more than one language in the same year, high five them for thinking big but suggest they pick one to start. If the first year goes well and you accomplish all your small goals, you can choose more challenging goals the second time around.

Aside from these three things, I really don't think I would change anything else. However, remember that my family is different from yours. You will probably need to modify more than what I just mentioned.

DIFFERENT, BRILLIANT STRATEGIES

As I've mentioned before, this roadmap is entirely customizable. In fact, every person I know that has used this roadmap has altered it in some way. They kept the framework the same, but they tweaked its execution. Not only do I support this, I encourage this. I know absolutely nothing about you or your family; all I know is that the basic framework of this roadmap is effective. I advise you take the same steps, but execute them however you see best fit. Hopefully, my personal experience served as a solid example of one way you can follow this roadmap. But to help you understand other ways you can execute this roadmap, I'd love to walk you through some of my friends' examples. To respect their privacy, I am going to use fake names.

When I told my really good friend Nick about this roadmap, he was eager to follow it with his wife Michelle. They don't have any kids yet, but Michelle is four months pregnant. Nick felt that if he completed Part One of the roadmap with Michelle before the baby was born, they could strengthen their relationship and become better parents. However, he didn't want to initiate the conversation with two worksheets. He was worried that Michelle might not like them, so he wanted to use a more creative and fun approach.

Have you ever seen the Duck/Rabbit illusion? It's an illustration that looks like both a duck and rabbit (I personally think it looks more like a duck, but Rachel thinks it looks more like a rabbit). Nick printed out a picture of this illusion and handed it to his wife one night. He simply asked her: "What is this a picture of?"

"Umm ... A duck?" Michelle replied.

"Really?! That's not what I see..." he said.

"What do you mean? What else could it be?"

"I think it's a rabbit," he stated. Michelle looked back at the photo.

"Oh my gosh, I would have never noticed the rabbit if you didn't say that!" They both laughed.

"Isn't it funny that we can look at the same exact thing, but see it totally differently?"

"Yeah, it's pretty bizarre," she replied.

"It just shows that everyone has their own unique perspectives, which is why I wanted to show you this," Nick explained. "If we can perceive the same things differently, don't you think we should talk about how we see things? It's really the only way to make sure we're on the same page."

"Yeah, that makes sense," she replied. With that being said, he pulled out the worksheets. He told her that the worksheets would reveal how they both perceived the past. As soon as they completed them together, he called me to tell me "Thank you." They ended up talking about their views and opinions for hours, and they even brought up things they've been avoiding for the past five years. He said there were a few tears from past issues not resolved but the wall they both had built up started to come down.

If you think Nick's optical illusion approach would be effective with your spouse, feel free to try it out. Your conversation probably won't go exactly like Nick and Michelle's, but you can still make the same point at the end. Explain that you're curious how each of you perceived this past year, and mention that the worksheets will help you both find out.

***

One day when I was having lunch with my friend Ryan, he randomly asked me, "So what's up with this roadmap you created?" I had told very few people about the roadmap at that point, so I was really surprised he heard about it somehow.

"How did you hear about that?" I replied.

"Josh from our EO group mentioned it to me," he answered. "He said he thinks it sounds like a great idea and I should ask you more about it. Needless to say, I've been dying to find out more. So, what is it?!"

I spent the next ten minutes or so explaining the issues I was having with my family and the roadmap to him. He didn't interrupt me once while I talked; he just listened closely and looked at me very intently. Once I was finally done, I asked him what he thought.

"I absolutely love it! The whole roadmap is so simple, so clever and practical. But unfortunately, I don't think it would work for my family, especially the goals-planning part. My wife *hates* setting goals and making plans; she doesn't really believe in that kind of business stuff."

"Wait a minute. If your wife doesn't believe in goals and planning, what *does* she believe in?" I asked. I am a very goals-oriented person, so I could hardly fathom this.

"She's a big believer in living in the moment. She loves to relax, meditate and enjoy the little things in life. In fact, she tells me all the time that I need to stop worrying about the future."

As soon as Ryan finished explaining this, his reservations made complete sense to me. If a person is dedicated to living in the moment, they have no reason to set goals! If Ryan really wanted to use this roadmap with his wife and kids, he would need to modify it a bit.

For the next twenty minutes or so, Ryan and I brainstormed alternatives to the dream board and goals planning activity. After throwing around some really dumb and terrible ideas, especially after a few cocktails, we finally came up with a brilliant one. When Ryan later explained the modified roadmap to his wife, she was instantly onboard. They ended up completing the retreat a few months later, and they've been a lot happier ever since.

Instead of creating dream boards on the third day of the retreat, Ryan and his family created Stuff We Love (SWL) boards. Rather than finding photos of things they wanted to accomplish or attain, they picked out photos of things that they simply love. The pictures and words on their boards portrayed their hobbies, values, loved ones, favorite foods, and anything else that brings them immense joy. To ensure that their boards were well-balanced, they included items for each of the three main areas of their lives: personal, professional and family.

Once they were done, they presented their boards to each other and explained why the things they chose make them really happy. Afterwards, Tyler asked his wife, "How about this next year, we make all of these positive things more apparent in our lives? We can even spend some time every month reviewing these boards so that we don't forget." His wife absolutely loved the idea. As a result, Ryan was able to avoid setting goals with his family while still setting his family up for future success.

When I asked Ryan if the SWL boards are benefiting his family, he ranted on about how valuable they are. They even framed them and hung them on the wall. The boards help his family focus on the things that make them truly happy, which is motivating them to attain more of these things. They also help him remember that life isn't all about work; it's about enjoying the journey and experiencing what fulfills you. Finally, studying everyone else's boards makes it easier for Ryan to make better decisions for his family. By knowing and remembering what his family members love, he can identify what actions will increase everyone's happiness.

If you or your spouse don't believe in setting goals, I definitely recommend using Ryan's approach. Instead of creating dream boards or a goals spreadsheet, build SWL boards that you reference regularly. If you *don't* make this adjustment, you'll be pressuring someone to be something they aren't—and that could get ugly really quickly. Just accept each other for who you are, and modify the roadmap so that it respects everyone's life philosophies.

Believe it or not, the SWL boards are also ideal for couples who are *crazy* goal-setters. Maybe you and your spouse have already planned out the entire next year together, or maybe you've already created some type of vision board. If that's the case, great! But I bet there's a good chance that the goals you've set together don't keep the journey in mind. They guarantee that you will be more accomplished, but they don't guarantee that you will be happy as you pursue those accomplishments. A SWL board can change that.

Although SWL boards make it more difficult to plan out actionable next steps, it can still provide you and your family with immense value. Most importantly, a SWL board will help you realize and remember what makes your life truly worth living. Whether it features certain moments, people, places or things, this board helps you focus on what most fulfills you and brings you joy. This way, you can make sure your life stays headed in the right direction and better realize when you're veering off track. After all, if you don't know what makes you and your family truly happy, it will be impossible to enhance your happiness.

As a side note, you should realize that you can still create your own family goals even if you don't create the dream boards or goals spreadsheet with your family. Just because your family isn't interested in creating and completing goals, that doesn't mean *you* shouldn't be. If you want to set some goals for yourself that will help you strengthen your family, just do so after the retreat! Once you learn how everyone felt about the past year and figure out what they love most in life, establishing your own secret family goals should be easy. For example, let's say everyone in your family mentioned that they didn't like how much you worked last year. During their SWL board presentations, they also mentioned that they love watching movies. As a result, you establish a goal to watch movies at home more often. This way, you can spend less time working and more time enjoying what everyone loves.

Just remember that if you establish your own family goals, you'll need to hold yourself accountable. Track your progress on these goals every month or so, and modify them when they don't seem to be working out. If you do this successfully, you can improve your family life without requiring anyone else to commit to goals.

WHAT HAPPENS NOW

Have you ever had an employee who pitched an idea to you before they fully thought it through? I certainly have, and the conversation usually goes over about the same way every time. One of these situations happened to me just a few months ago. I was sitting in my office when one of my employees popped his head in. He asked if he could talk to me about something for a minute, so I invited him in.

After he sat down, he excitedly said, "I think I have a really great idea!"

"Awesome, I love great ideas!" I happily replied. "Let's hear it."

"Well last night I was doing some research, and I came across this social media campaign that General Electric is running on Twitter. It's basically a bunch of pictures of their employees holding up signs that say why they love working for the company. I know we're trying to hire more people, so I thought maybe we could do something similar!"

He pulled up General Electric's Twitter feed and showed me what he was talking about. I thought it was an awesome campaign, but I didn't understand how it could work for us.

"I mean yeah, that's a great idea! But General Electric is trying to hire very different people than we are. They also have a really well-known social media presence and hundreds of employees to showcase, which isn't true for us," I pointed out. "So, why do you think something like this would be effective for us?"

"Oh, those are really good points.... Sorry, it probably isn't a good idea then. I should have thought it through more," he concluded. I could tell by the sound of his voice that he felt foolish and was disappointed in himself. I told him not to worry about it and thanked him for being on the lookout for new opportunities. I made sure he knew that I love hearing his ideas; it's just my job to challenge them.

When you finish reading this book, you may be tempted to run up to your spouse and declare, "Honey, I think we should use this roadmap!" But if you do, there's a good chance you'll end up feeling just like my employee: foolish and disappointed. Why? Because you skipped the first and most important step of the roadmap! You didn't consider why you believe in it, or why it is right for your family. Once your partner starts asking you questions about it, you won't know the answers. As a result, getting him or her onboard will be almost impossible.

Once you finish reading this book, avoid rushing into anything. Instead, take your time and go through the first step of the roadmap first. As I mentioned in the beginning of this book, the first step of this roadmap is to take a long, hard look at yourself in the mirror. You must understand who you are, where your family is, and where you want to be. Decide if you're truly willing to follow this roadmap and why. After all, if you don't believe in this roadmap, why should anyone else?

****

"ONCE YOU FINISH READING THIS BOOK, AVOID RUSHING INTO ANYTHING. INSTEAD, TAKE YOUR TIME AND GO THROUGH THE FIRST STEP OF THE ROADMAP FIRST."

****

To get through this first step successfully, here are some questions to consider:

- Why do I want to reboot or improve my family?
- What exactly do I want to change or improve in my family?
- How am I currently holding myself and my family back from achieving the life I want for us?
- Am I willing to change my mindset, behaviors and actions in order to improve my family?
- Why do I want to follow this roadmap?
- Why is this roadmap right for my family?
- Am I willing to sacrifice a portion of my time and energy to pursue this roadmap?

- Am I willing to be honest with my family once we start following this roadmap?
- Why should each of my family members be willing to follow this roadmap?
- How do I need to modify this roadmap for my family?

Once you know the answers to these questions, you'll be better prepared to propose this roadmap to your spouse. You will be able to confidently answer questions about it, accurately explain how it works, and describe what it can do for your family. You'll also know for certain that you're willing to do what it takes to reboot your family, which will allow you to sound more believable and persuasive. Plus, you would never want to suggest something that you actually aren't willing to do.

DECISION TIME

If you've made it this far into the book, there must be a part of you that seriously wants to improve your family life. Otherwise, why did you read this entire book? If it was just because you know or like me, well... that's very flattering! But I didn't write this book to improve my image. I wrote this book to help other entrepreneurs and business executives improve their family lives. If you're a businessperson, I need your help. Help this book serve its true purpose by improving your family.

If you're an entrepreneur or a business executive, you're probably aware that complaining and fantasizing will get you nowhere in your career. In order to become the professional you want to be, you must pursue solutions and actualize your potential. You need to put in ample amounts of time and effort to produce spectacular results. You must overcome challenges to strengthen yourself, and step out of your comfort zone to stretch yourself. You can't be passive or complacent; you need to be bold and keep moving forward.

I hope that by this point, you've come to realize that this same logic applies to your family. If this is how you perceive the business world, maintain this perspective when you're at home too. Don't complain about your family problems and wish that things were better. It's a waste of time and energy, and it gets you absolutely nowhere. Instead, do what it takes to improve your family life. Be willing to fight for what you love and believe in, at all times and in every setting.

If you're still doubting yourself, now is the time to stop. Instead, feel confident in knowing what you're capable of. You already had what it takes to strengthen your family before you started reading this book. You just didn't realize that you could apply these skills at home. But now you do, and you understand exactly how to these skills can be applied. Now, no matter whether you're at work or at home, you can effectively initiate change, communicate with others, and take something to the next level. You have the drive, passion and willpower required to scale both a business and a family. You have everything it takes, and all of the insights you need. You are fully capable of enhancing every area of your life.

You also have all the tools you need to effectively execute these skills. I've given you various techniques, strategies, worksheets, and activities so that you can reboot your family. And let's not forget the obvious—I gave you an entire roadmap! While I don't expect you to implement absolutely everything I've suggested, I hope you walk away with at least a few tools that you're eager to start using. In fact, I encourage you to make a list of your key takeaways from this book so that you can remember what parts resonated with you most. Maybe some of the activities I explained really stood out to you, or perhaps I gave you some pointers that you knew would be helpful later on. Whatever your key takeaways are, write them down somewhere safe so you won't forget them.

However, writing them down won't be enough. If you want to improve your family, you also need to put these key takeaways into action. You need to leverage the skills and tools you've gained from this book and start pursuing the life you want. You must initiate hard conversations with yourself and your family, and begin exploring potential solutions. This is the only way you'll finally get out of the rut you're in and experience a more fulfilling life. You'll even be able to achieve happiness—true happiness—as long you put everything you've learned and gained into action.

But remember, if you speak up and initiate change, your life won't be the only one that's transformed for the better. You will also enhance the lives of everyone in your family. If you're questioning whether or not you want to use this roadmap, think about your family and their happiness. Because if you do follow these steps, you aren't doing it just for yourself. You're doing it for the people that you love, and for the chance to empower everyone to reach their true potential. Speak up not only for yourself, but for everyone else. This is your chance to be a hero.

At the end of the day though, it's entirely your choice. I can't make you do anything; I can only make suggestions as to what I believe you should do. It's up to you to decide what happens now. You can choose to remain unfulfilled and frustrated, or you can choose to elevate your family life. If you want to make the right choice, consider what you want to attain first. And I know you want more than just a rewarding career—you want a loving family and fulfilling life. Otherwise, what's the point of all this hard work?

ABOUT THE AUTHOR

In 2010, Arizona entrepreneur Jay Feitlinger launched his 8th company: StringCan Interactive, a digital marketing agency. StringCan, with offices in Scottsdale, Arizona and Paris, France, drives business growth for multi-location businesses by attracting, converting and retaining their most profitable customers.

Jay has been married for 15 years and is raising two daughters with his wife Rachel. Applying the StringCan "connect smart" approach to work-life balance, Jay found himself asking, "Why can't we connect better when engaging with family members and grow our own family relationships?" Like most families, Jay and his family have their challenges—most of which are tied to communication. Jay used what has worked well in his businesses to identify how he could strengthen his own family.

Jay ultimately transformed business best practices into a four-day, family-friendly retreat. While on this retreat, his family talked about respect, reflected on the past year ups and downs, established family goals for the coming year, and of course—had a lot of fun together. As a result, his family (and others who have completed the Family 2.0 process) have never been stronger! For entrepreneurs and business executives who desire more out of their family lives, Jay will share his Family 2.0 retreat process in this book. He shares the challenges he faced balancing family and work, along with the solutions he has created, in order to help other entrepreneurs, thrive in their personal lives as well.

You can connect with Jay:

Email: jay.feitlinger@gmail.com

Twitter: www.twitter.com/jayfeitlinger

LinkedIn: www.linkedin.com/in/jayfeitlinger/

Website Personal: www.jayfeitlinger.com

Website Business: www.stringcaninteractive.com